Writing News
for Broadcast

Writing News for Broadcast

Third Edition

Edward Bliss, Jr.
James L. Hoyt

Columbia University Press
New York

Columbia University Press
New York   Chichester, West Sussex
Copyright © 1994 Columbia University Press
All rights reserved

Library of Congress Cataloging-in-Publication Data

Bliss, Edward, 1912–
    Writing news for broadcast / Ed Bliss, Jr., James L. Hoyt—3d
ed.
        p.   cm.
    Includes bibliographical references and index.
    ISBN 0–231–07972–9
    ISBN 0–231–07973–7 (pbk.)
    1. Broadcast journalism—Authorship.   I. Hoyt, James L.
II. Title.
PN4784.B75B55   1994
808'.06607—dc20

                                                    93–29715
                                                    CIP

∞

Printed in the United States of America
c 10 9 8 7 6 5 4 3 2 1
p 10 9 8 7 6 5 4 3 2 1

To the memory of
Edward R. Murrow

Contents

Acknowledgments

For examples of good writing, we are indebted to the major networks—ABC, CBS, NBC, CNN, and PBS. Local stations also contributed, and we are grateful to KDKA-TV, Pittsburgh; WCNC-TV, Charlotte, and WISC-TV, Madison. There are individuals we must thank, including Mervin Block, Rita Braver, David Brinkley, Walter Cronkite, Joseph Dembo, James Esser, John Hart, Charlayne Hunter-Gault, Kenneth Middleton, Bruce Morton, Deborah Potter, Andy Rooney, Morley Safer, Dick Schaap, Bernard Shaw, Emerson Stone, and Ann Utterback. Special appreciation goes to Janet Murrow, who helped make available excerpts from her late husband's broadcasts. We also are grateful for the patience, as well as guidance, accorded us by Ann M. Miller, associate executive editor at Columbia University Press. We thank Bill Bramlette for the painstaking job he did as manuscript editor.

We recall with affection, as well as appreciation, that it was Fred W. Friendly who, in 1969, when no such text existed, said this book should be written.

Introduction

As before, this third edition is designed for broadcast journalists, present and future. We have wanted to create something that both working journalists and students would find helpful. John Patterson, who co-authored the first edition, lived to see adoption of the book in scores of newsrooms. That pleased him. He took acceptance by professionals as the highest compliment. Again, our goal is to provide useful guidelines; there are few ironclad rules.

In broadcast journalism writing is still basic. Whether reporters are broadcasting from Beijing or Baghdad, or from an uplink in the Mojave Desert, they usually are reading what they have written. Often they have less than two minutes to tell their story. A special economy of language, a most sophisticated kind of editorial judgment, is required if, in that short time, they are to report the essential—the undistorted essence—of what took place. The story must be told as lucidly as possible, because the audience has to understand at once what it hears—there is no going back to listen again. Writing for broadcast demands a style that is comely and clean.

Artistry is involved.

There are, in today's newscasts, too many clunking phrases and illiterate sentences. Too many bromides. Vernon Stone, professor emeritus, University of Missouri, says "Literacy has been eroding in the medium that holds such potential for education by example." The writer of newscasts—one who is a *good* writer—respects language, knows grammar, and knows how to write with exactness and grace. Moreover, this good writer knows the importance of how a phrase or a sentence sounds. A great editor of NBC News, Gilbert Millstein, said, "I have discovered that, properly done—and I cannot emphasize it too strongly, PROPERLY DONE—

TV newswriting is indeed the clearest and most economical way of telling people what is happening and why.''

That is the challenge for students entering the field of broadcast journalism and for the men and women already in it. The challenge is great because the spoken word is so perishable, time is so short, and the picture on occasion so misleading. Students should realize that, even in television news, writing in most instances is the key element. And surely students who are graduating should know the market is tight.

But the situation is not hopeless. Each year sees more syndicated news and information services, more cable systems offering news. CNN is thriving, and some local cable companies have gone all-news. There has been an explosion in the number of state and regional news services. Wire services have expanded their broadcast operations. And now the telephone companies are getting into the act.

All these services are looking for people who can write. *Really write*. If you can write grammatically and with grace, and if you want to work in broadcasting—and love news—hang in there. You can make it. If you do not have the ability, and the love, it would be well to look somewhere else.

The first text on broadcast newswriting was *News on the Air,* written by Paul W. White in 1947. White directed CBS's coverage of World War II and taught at Columbia University's Graduate School of Journalism. He wrote the book in plain language, and for instruction he often used historic events. In this third edition of *Writing News for Broadcast* we have tried to follow his example in both respects, although not to the extent of excluding local, more mundane examples that may prove instructive.

Of necessity, the practitioners of broadcast journalism created a new verbal form. The challenge in preparing this third edition, as with earlier editions, has been to make clear what the new form requires.

E. B., Jr.

J. L. H.

1. *A New Way of Reporting*

In the beginning, when it was called wireless, most radio news consisted of weather forecasts and grain futures. Other news items taken from newspapers crept in, and broadcasters began amending the language of print because, after all, they were speaking.

In 1920 a Pittsburgh station, KDKA, went on the air to report the returns in the presidential election in which Warren G. Harding defeated James M. Cox. The voice of Lowell Thomas became as well known as the voice of the president of the United States. A king abdicated the throne of England—on radio. And almost continuously for eighteen days in 1938, H. V. Kaltenborn analyzed Prime Minister Chamberlain's nightmarish talks with Hitler seeking "peace in our time." And when war did come, radio news came of age.

The role of radio in that time—the role of words heard simultaneously by millions—cannot be measured. Eric Sevareid observed

> Never, surely, in the history of human travail had so many owed so much to so few human voices. . . . Churchill speaking to the world. J. B. Priestley speaking to his own people. Ed Murrow speaking to America each night, the timbre of his powerful, steady voice reflecting the spirit of England and persuading millions of Americans that the cause was not lost even when it seemed beyond saving. Raymond Swing speaking from America to the British via the BBC each week, letting them know in his intimate fatherly tones that America had got their message, that America understood.

What were the words of these men? How did they write? Here is an excerpt from a Murrow script, vintage 1940:

Christmas Day began in London nearly an hour ago. The church bells did not ring at midnight. When they ring again it will be to announce invasion. And if they ring, the British are ready. Tonight, as on every other night, the rooftop watchers are peering out across the fantastic forest of London's chimney pots. The anti-aircraft gunners stand ready. And all along the coast of this island the observers revolve in their reclining chairs, listening for the sound of German planes. The fire fighters and the ambulance drivers are waiting, too. The blackout stretches from Birmingham to Bethlehem, but tonight over Britain the skies are clear.

This is writing news for broadcast. The sentences are readable. They are short and to the point. There is no fancy, involved writing. No "inverted pyramid" with the answers to who, what, when, why, where, and how crammed into the first couple of sentences. The style is simple and straightforward. This is copy written to be read aloud, to be heard once and, with only that one hearing, to be understood.

For years it has been the habit of teachers of journalism to illustrate broadcast style by comparing it with the style of writing found in newspapers. So will the authors of the present text, but only in passing. The writing found in newspapers today increasingly resembles the writing in news broadcasts, so that the comparison—still interesting—is less relevant.

Here are the leads to four stories that appeared January 24, 1992, in the *New York Times*. After you have read them, let's see how they might be rewritten for radio or television.

WASHINGTON—The Government said today that claims for jobless benefits surged in the second week of January by about 46,000 from the previous week.

BONN—The German Parliament, embarrassed by new disclosures that German companies supplied Iraq with equipment that could be used to build nuclear weapons, approved long-stalled legislation today tightening controls on arms exports.

SEOUL—The United States has given North Korea a deadline for allowing inspections of its nuclear sites and will propose that an American air base be opened simultaneously, the South Korean news agency reported today.

SEATTLE—Reaching to Japan in an effort to keep the American national pastime alive in Seattle, this city's leaders announced today that a group led by Japanese investors had made an offer to buy the Seattle Mariners baseball team for $100 million.

Of these four leads, only the first is right for broadcast. It is written pretty nearly as you would speak. Two observations, however. In a radio or TV script, "46,000" would be written "46-thousand." And it strikes us that "unemployment benefits" is a better phrase than "jobless benefits." The benefits are not jobless.

The lead from Bonn is too long. Researchers have found listeners often have trouble absorbing information in sentences of more than twenty words. This sentence has thirty-òne words, not too many for a newspaper, but remember you are writing for the ear, not the eye. There's a limit to the information you can give all at once. Moreover, the listeners' comprehension is further hampered by the placement of nineteen words between subject and verb. For a newscast, this lead should be broken up into two sentences so it reads something like this:

> Today the German parliament finally approved legislation tightening the controls on arms exports. Members were embarrassed by new disclosures that German companies sold Iraq equipment it could use for nuclear weapons.

Moral: Beware of long sentences If you have one, try putting the information in two sentences, or three.

The lead datelined Seoul breaks the first commandment in broadcast newswriting: Thou shalt not dangle attribution. In broadcast reporting, as in conversation, you put the attribution up front. You would never tell anyone what the United States reportedly was doing and then, at the end of the sentence, tack on "the South Korean news agency reported today." Write as you would speak in civil conversation. In this respect, broadcast writing should be the easiest, most natural writing imaginable.

The other difficulty with this lead is that it asks the listener to absorb the fact that a deadline has been set for U.S. inspection of North Korean nuclear sites, and, in the same sentence, the fact that the United States will make some kind of proposal about an air base. That is asking too much. Many listeners won't get it. Besides, just what does "opening" the air base mean? In this instance, it means allowing North Korean inspection of the base where, according to rumor, nuclear warheads were stored. That has to be brought out.

So what we need here is more than one sentence and some clarification. Strive, always, for clarity. The lead, revised for broadcast, might read

> There's a report that the United States has given North Korea a deadline for allowing inspection of its atomic sites. The report comes from the South Korean news agency. It says if the deadline is met, the United States may let North Korea inspect an American base in South Korea, so it can see that the nuclear warheads said to be stored there have indeed been removed.

Because the story is complicated, we used three sentences, one piece of the story to each sentence. We resisted two temptations. One was not to identify the source of the report—it would have made the lead simpler—but identification seemed important. It helps listeners judge the authenticity of the report. And did we have to say the American base was in South Korea? We decided we did, though the writer of the original lead did not. Many listeners would guess the base was located in South Korea, but they should not have to guess. We made two small changes. We didn't think it necessary to identify the base as an air base, and in the first sentence we changed the word *inspections* to *inspection*. In your writing, eliminate every superfluous *s*. They make for slippery reading on the air.

The Seattle lead is easier to fix. Begin by killing the first 15 words. In broadcast news, leads don't start with long participial phrases. They start with the what, not with the why. For radio and television, the lead might be

> The Japanese, who have invested billions of dollars in American business, are bidding for a major league baseball team, the Seattle Mariners. Japanese investors have offered to buy the Mariners for 100 million dollars. The offer looks good because the club has run into hard times, and Seattle wants to keep the franchise.

We put the Mariners story in perspective by referring to previous Japanese investments. Nothing says that in rewriting you can't embellish. Again, each facet of the story rates a separate sentence. (Good practice, but not a hard-and-fast rule. And notice that *$100 million* becomes *100 million dollars*. Your script should conform to what you are going to say on the air. In print, the dollar sign comes first, but in broadcast copy the word *dollar* comes last because that's where it comes when you speak.

All these leads from the *Times* can be rewritten for broadcast in other ways. You may want to see what you can do with them. Every piece of writing can be improved.

Dan Enright, producer of many of television's early game shows, died on May 22, 1992. An example of how *not* to write for broadcast is this sentence from the obituary in the *New York Times:*

> He was 74 years old and died after a brief illness, a family spokesman said, the Associated Press reported.

For broadcast, eliminate the clumsy, dangling double attribution. Instead of *he,* repeat the name of the deceased. Recall your own frustration when, having missed a name, all you hear are references to *he, she, him, her*. Lastly, it probably would be a good idea to consign the two bits of information—age and length of illness—to two sentences. So the broadcast version might read

> The Associated Press says he had been ill only a short time. Dan Enright was 74.

Should we have left out reference to the family spokesman? You may want to discuss that.

Came the Revolution

At one time newspapers were written in an ornate, pretentious style for which the chief rule seems to have been to make sentences as long and convoluted as possible while, at the same time, stuffing them with more facts than they could decently hold. Consider this tortured lead that appeared in the *New York Times,* issue of July 30, 1912:

> Lieut. Charles A. Becker, the one-time head of Police Commissioner Waldo's strong arm squad, whose name has been mentioned in connection with the case ever since Herman Rosenthal, the gambler who had threatened to "squeal," was murdered in front of the Hotel Metropole last July 16, was arrested last night, immediately indicted for murder in the first degree and locked in the Tombs, there to await a further hearing a week from yesterday.

This kind of lead appeared frequently in the nineteenth and early twentieth centuries. Since then all newspaper writing has become simpler and clearer, and broadcasting exerted an important, unpublicized influence in bringing this about.

An arbitrary, arguable date can be set for the beginning of radio's part in this transformation. The Second World War had entered its seventh month, and stations and networks were filling their schedules with news for a public hungry for word from the battlefronts. It was recognized that writing for radio—for the ear—differed from writing for newspapers—for the eye—and various notions were held on how best to adapt. CBS's Paul White decided his writers needed a stylebook, and on March 3, 1941, he posted a memorandum asking them for suggestions.

Responses trickled in to White all through the next week. One staff member called the idea of a stylebook ridiculous. "There can be no instructions per se for radio newswriting," he said. "You either have a flair for doing that sort of thing or you haven't." Replying to this "surprisingly bad-tempered and somewhat boorish memorandum," White said:

> There certainly *can* be instructions per se for radio newswriting. I should hate to be responsible for a news department whose members were able to write anything they pleased in any manner they pleased. Even worse, I should hate to be the listener.

The result was a small stylebook titled *Radio News Writing,* which starts by asking "Is it listenable?" and ends with "The chief responsibility of desk men is to make radio news so clear that it will prevent call-backs from listeners who have been confused."

Listenability and clarity.

Three years later, White called on his staff to cooperate in an experiment being conducted by the International News Service (INS). This news-gathering organization, owned by William Randolph Hearst, had no broadcast wire. It wanted its regular press wire to be written in such a way that it could serve its radio clients as well as newspapers. Network writers were asked to check the INS copy and suggest how to make it more readable—more listenable.

This was done. INS issued a brochure saying that henceforth its stories would be written in a "modern, simplified style." Research, it said, had "found that, rather than a conflict, there was a close relationship between writing for the eye and for the ear." INS boasted that, as a result, its news wire had been restyled to make it "easier to read, easier to broadcast, easier to understand."

At the same time, the United Press made a study of its news reports. When the study was completed, Earl Johnson, UP's general manager, issued a memorandum that said in part: "Much of the news these days is of such vital importance that it deserves to be presented in terms that can be understood by the widest possible audience. Let's have more periods and fewer complex words. Watch that lead sentence. Keep it short and simple. Then let the lead set the pace for the whole piece."

A similar campaign against obfuscation took place at the Associated Press. Everywhere, what the INS brochure described as "the 1890-style hangover" was being discarded. Even the good, gray *New York Times* began publishing stories that were "easier to read, easier to understand," so that when Astronauts Neil Armstrong and Edwin "Buzz" Aldrin landed on the moon, John Noble Wilford of the *Times* wrote this historic lead:

> HOUSTON, July 20—Men landed on the moon today.

It is difficult to imagine a clearer, more concise, more readable lead sentence.

The revolution—evolution, really—in news style is continuing. Throwbacks to earlier, unnatural journalese still occur, although rarely is the language as tortured as that found in the reporting of Lieutenant Becker's indictment in 1912. Here, for comparison, are more recent examples taken from two leading American newspapers. The *New York Times* version:

> The discovery in mountains near the South Pole of the fossil remains of a reptilian counterpart of the hippopotamus that lived, as well, in Africa has established "beyond further question" the former joining of all the southern continents, according to a leading authority on the subject.

The lead for the same story as it appeared in the *Washington Post:*

> Scientists have found a 200-million-year-old reptile skull in Antarctica that they said "establishes without further question" that the earth once consisted of one or two continents that split into the present seven.

The *Washington Post* lead is more conversational in structure, and it is interesting to note that the writer, Stuart Auerbach—whether consciously or not—adhered to broadcast style in writing the figure 200,000,000 as 200 million for easy comprehension.

None of this is meant to suggest that newspapers never would have clarified their language if it had not been for broadcast journalists. However, broadcast journalism did have a direct effect. As Paul White said, "It wasn't until radio really got going that news reached Americans in simple, direct English." It created a new style for writing news.

The Eyewitness Medium

What about television? Television added the picture to the word. At its best, television shows history as it is happening. In covering a tragedy such as the assassination of President Kennedy, or a triumph, such as man's first walk on the moon, television journalism is unsurpassed. "Seeing," as the *New York Times* observed during the mission of Apollo 11, "is still believing." Television not only records history; it changes history. It was America becoming eyewitness to war, through television, that helped build up public revulsion against the Vietnam War. And television has revolutionized politics.

But seeing is not always understanding; ideas and issues are not easily shown. Watch the evening news and notice how many words are spoken by the anchorperson, by staff reporters, and by people—public officials, witnesses at congressional hearings, visiting dignitaries, and so forth—who made the day's news. If you turn off the picture, you would miss only one or two of the stories reported in the entire half-hour.

But in most television journalism, word and picture are complementary. Each reinforces the other. It might be said that the best television news programs are those in which voice and picture, combined, produce revelation, new insight—truth.

Television owes its life to both microphone *and* camera, to sound as well as to sight. You hear natural sounds—traffic noises, grenades exploding, a dog barking—and you hear human voices, some wise, some foolish, and these voices speak in words. Respect the word.

With well-chosen words the radio reporter can make the listener see in the minds' eye what is happening. Note how, in this report on the German blitz against London, Ed Murrow used words that help the listener, visually, share his experience:

> Up toward London we could see billows of smoke fanning out above the river and, over our heads, the British fighters climbing almost straight up, trying to intercept the bombers before they got away. It went on for two hours, and then the all-clear. . . . Before eight the sirens sounded again. We went back to a haystack near the airdrome. The fires up the

river had turned the moon blood-red. The smoke had drifted down until it formed a canopy over the Thames. The guns were working all around us, the bursts looking like fireflies in a Southern summer night.

As World War II began, *Variety* said, "Murrow in London always gets close to the dramatic and human element, and furnishes an account which is clear and to the point." There could be no better dictum for the correspondent for radio or television: Be clear and to the point.

Clarity was the hallmark of Murrow's writing. His leads were simple, short, declarative sentences. The sentences in the body of his broadcasts were often written in the same simple, direct style. Here are the first two paragraphs of Murrow's broadcast of April 22, 1945, reporting the fall of Leipzig to American troops:

"Tell them resistance was slight!" That's what a GI shouted to us as we entered Leipzig. There were two tankers dead at the corner. Somebody had covered them with a blanket. There was a sniper working somewhere in the next block. Four boys went out to deal with him, then there was silence.

The Gestapo headquarters had been evacuated in a great hurry, but they had taken all their files with them. Down in the air raid shelter the floor was covered with money—Belgian, Polish, Hungarian—wherever the Germans had been. The money was ankle deep, and it was dirty. And it had no meaning.

This is eyewitness reporting of the first order, comparable to Murrow's descriptions of the Battle of Britain and his firsthand account of the bombing of Berlin. The writing is dramatic, but without dramatics. No fancy words are used, almost no adjectives. When an adjective *is* used, it is used with telling effect. For example, with reference to the money: [and it was] *dirty*. Here is an excerpt of Murrow's report on the liberation of the wretched inmates of Buchenwald.

Men and boys reached out to touch me. They were in rags and the remnants of uniforms. Death had already marked many of them, but they were smiling with their eyes. . . . When I reached the center of the barracks, a man came up and said, "You remember me. I'm Peter Zenkl, onetime mayor of Prague." I remembered him but did not recognize him. . . . I asked how many men had died in that building during the last month. They called the doctor. We inspected his records. There were only names in the little black book, nothing more—nothing of who these men were, what they had done, or hoped. Behind the names of those who had died there was a cross. I counted them. They totaled 242—242 out of 1200 in one month. As I walked down to the end of the barracks, there was applause from the men too weak to get out of bed. It sounded like the handclapping of babies, they were so weak.

Edward Weeks, the great editor of the *Atlantic,* said of Murrow: "His manliness and compassion were never more touching than in his broadcast on Buchenwald, spoken the day that President Roosevelt died, and in his tribute to the British on V-E Day, ending with these poignant words: 'Some people appear not to be part of the celebration. Their minds must be filled with memories of friends who died in the streets where they now walk, and of others who have died from Burma to the Elbe. There are a few men on crutches, as though to remind all that there is much human wreckage left at the end. Six years is a long time. I have observed today that people have very little to say. There are no words.' "

Of Murrow's style of writing, Weeks said it was vivid. And he said "the timing was such that he had to be economical, and he favored the understatement." Then the magazine editor—no broadcaster—made one of the best judgments of what good writing for broadcast journalism is by saying "Broadcasting is writing for the mind through the ear, and it is quite different from writing for the eye, a distinction not always appreciated by professors [!]. Sentences must be short; words with a high vowel content make a much sharper impact. Consonants are likely to fluff and be missed. And the sentence structure must accentuate one image or one idea, not an assortment."

During World War II no one wrote for Murrow. He wrote for himself. However, with the start of the nightly radio program "Edward R. Murrow and the News" in 1947, he was assisted in his writing chores by Jesse Zousmer, a CBS News editor. For the next eight years Zousmer wrote the hard news that made up the first six or seven minutes of the program, while Murrow wrote an analysis, or commentary, filling out the rest of the fifteen-minute broadcast. The program received more awards than any other news program in the history of radio, and Zousmer was recognized as the best news writer in the business. (He died in a plane crash in 1966.)

Zousmer's news summaries, of classically simple design, can be taken as models today. The sentences are lean, almost completely devoid of adjectives. Verbs are active. The language is conversational, yet never chatty. One searches in vain for exaggeration—no impression is given of knowing everything. Sources, where necessary, are identified.

Here is a sample, written on January 17, 1951, during the first year of the Korean War. For its clear language, this is a classic news summary. Notice its flow.

> Communist China has rejected the United Nations' peace plan. The Communists have offered their own plan. The United States calls it unacceptable. In a few minutes I'd like to review these developments and where they leave us now.
>
> In Korea, according to the reports available to us, things are very quiet. We have word of the enemy massing his troops below Seoul for a possible attack. Military sources are remembering that this type of lull preceded the Chinese attack in late November. But we are told only of

small patrol actions all along the 130-mile front. A late United Press dispatch says an Allied reconnaissance patrol entered Wonju late today and found it deserted.

In Indo-China, the French claim a great victory. They say Communist troops have fallen back north of Hanoi with "tremendous" casualties after four days of battle.

In Burma, Dr. Gordon Seagrave, the American doctor who is widely known as "the Burma surgeon," today was convicted of high treason and sentenced to six years in prison. Dr. Seagrave told reporters, "I sincerely hope the American people will not judge the people of Burma by the action of a few." He is appealing the decision.

In this country, a high government source (who doesn't want his name used) says we're going to have a freeze on prices and wages within the next week. Mobilization Chief Wilson is reported to have decided that voluntary controls just won't work. Mr. Wilson may explain his position in a speech he's making tonight to the Poor Richard Club in Philadelphia.

Another report from Washington has it that the soft coal industry has decided to give the miners a voluntary 20-cent-an-hour wage increase, with the consumer eventually paying for it through a price increase.

The auto industry told the government today that it's going to cut production 20 to 30 percent below last year's record of 8-million cars and trucks. That would mean the production of from five-and-a-half to six-and-a-half million vehicles.

The President said today he's going to try voluntary controls to get the most out of our available manpower. He said, "Each individual will be expected to serve in the capacity in which he can contribute the most to the total mobilization program." If this doesn't work out, the President will ask Congress for power to prevent "indiscriminate" shifts of workers from one job to another, power to say how many skilled workers an employer can hire, and power to compel employers to make full use of women and handicapped and minority groups.

Defense Secretary Marshall today formally asked Congress for permission to draft 18-year-olds. He promises that none of these boys will be sent into combat before they are 19, except in dire emergency. But he does *not* want a ban on sending 18-year-olds overseas. He feels that this would "cripple the services in meeting any sudden, ruthless and violent action by our enemy." Today, senators heard the heads of five colleges—M.I.T., Princeton, Tufts, Williams, and Johns Hopkins—support the draft of 18-year-olds.

The Air Force has suspended its recruiting, at least until the end of the month. Its basic training facilities are swamped.

Study this script. Note the simplicity of Zousmer's lead: ''Communist China has rejected the United Nations' peace plan.'' No adverbs. No adjectives except the one essential adjective *peace,* modifying the monosyllabic noun *plan,* which Zousmer chose over *proposal,* which is multisyllabic and takes three times as long to say. No fancy phrasing. No editorialization. Completely conversational. It's as though you are a newscaster, and a friend sees you on the elevator.

"What's new?" he asks.

And you say, "China's rejected the United Nations' peace plan."

Always think, when you write for broadcast, what you would *say.* Ask yourself how you would tell the story in your own words.

Notice the absence of triteness. After the foreign news—the war news from Korea and Indo-China—Zousmer leads off the first domestic story with the phrase *in this country,* eschewing the thin-worn phrase *here at home.* (Yes, it was thin-worn more than forty years ago!) The listener is oriented by the use of similar prepositional phrases: *in Korea, in Indo-China, in Burma.* Before Murrow reported the story, the listener knew where it happened. Such phrases act as datelines and enhance ease of understanding.

The lead story is told in the perfect tense. The next story from Korea is reported in the present tense. So is the story from Indo-China. But the report of Dr. Seagrave's conviction is told in the past tense. The tenses vary throughout the broadcast, avoiding monotony.

Note also the absence of verbal fat. Try excising words from Zousmer's script, and it will bleed. Vital elements will be lost.

A Difference in Appearance

In the last few pages, you have read—and, we hope, studied—some radio copy. The sentences had the same appearance, the same form, as the sentences you are reading now. Copy read in a television studio has a much different look. That is copy set up for a TelePrompTer, a device that permits the broadcaster to look into the camera and, at the same time, read the script from a small monitor mounted just above the lens.

Here's a sample. The story is the death of Superman, reported by Kathy Reilly for WCNC-TV, Charlotte, and this is how her script looked to Jesse Johnson on the Tele-Promp-Ter:

```
-(JESSE)----------
          COULD  IT
BE. .  COULD  THIS
BE  THE  END
FOR. . (PREGNANT-
PAUSE)-----------
      SUPERMAN??! !
```

THAT'S
RIGHT.
    THE MAN OF
STEEL IS GETTING
KNOCKED OFF.
 GOOD EVENING,
I'M JESSE
JOHNSON.
    THANKS FOR
JOINING FIRST
NEWS.
    YOU MAY
REMEMBER OR YOUR
CHILDREN MAY
READ ABOUT
SUPERMAN.
    YES, HE'S
ONLY A COMIC
BOOK
CHARACTER... BUT
HE'S A HERO.
WE DON'T HAVE
MANY OF THEM
THESE DAYS.
-----(FS)-------
NEWS 36'S KATHY
REILLY HAS OUR
TOP STORY ON THE
DEATH OF
SUPERMAN.

    JESSE,
IT'S A QUESTION
A LOT OF PEOPLE
WANT AN ANSWER
TO. SUPERMAN'S
A PART OF OUR
CULTURE. WE

GREW UP WITH THE
MAN FASTER THAN
A SPEEDING
BULLET,   MORE
POWERFUL THAN A
LOCOMOTIVE.
NOW, PEOPLE HERE
AT 'HEROES
AREN'T HARD TO
FIND' ARE LINING
UP TO READ ABOUT
YES, HIS DEATH.
--------(PKG)---
        SUPERMAN
FANS AND COMIC
BOOK COLLECTORS
AREN'T WAITING
AT ALL TO SNATCH
UP THEIR COPY OF
THE DEATH OF
SUPERMAN.
    HERE AT
'HEROES AREN'T
HARD TO FIND,'
THEY'RE LIMITING
IT TO ONE COPY
PER CUSTOMER...
TO AVOID A RUN
ON THE PLACE.
    THEIR
WAREHOUSE IS
FILLED WITH
THOUSANDS OF
COPIES,   BUT
THEY EXPECT TO
SELL OUT SOON.
    JESSE??

First of all, notice the tease. Although it's usually best not to start with a question, it works here. In this opening and what follows, the language, befitting a feature story, is highly informal. The simple, declarative sentences are short, averaging only eleven words in length.

The cleanliness of the language makes for easy listening. Yet the writer includes enough detail to make her story appealing—it's about this superhuman reporter for the *Daily Planet,* who is "faster than a speeding bullet and more powerful than a locomotive." This is a national story, but by going to a Charlotte bookstore the reporter made it a local story, too. And observe that, to report the death of a hero, she went to a bookstore with just the right name.

Reilly wrote her own lead-in, always a good idea. After all, the reporter knows best the thrust of the story.

There is a right way—Charles Osgood once called it "strategy"—for writing good broadcast copy. We take up that subject in the next chapter.

2. *Basic Work Rules*

Broadcast newswriting has a simple objective. That is to capture the essential ingredients of a story and explain them in straightforward, simple language that can be easily understood when heard over the air.

Just as there is no one correct broadcast newswriting style, there is no one correct set of work rules. This is not to say that such styles or rules don't exist. They clearly do, but they vary by station or by network.

Even if such styles and rules are occasionally violated—as almost all of them are—it is important for broadcast newswriters to know them, so they know when (and why) a rule or style is being violated.

The purpose of this book is to help you, in the specialized work of writing news for broadcast, to say what you have to say as clearly and effectively as possible. Two questions will be answered: What is effective writing in broadcast journalism? And how, by what devices, do you make your writing effective?

Before discussing these techniques, let's look at some basic work rules, which mostly have to do with format. They concern how you make up your script.

Not every newsroom prepares its copy the same way. In general, however, these rules hold. They are as basic to the process as turning on the ignition is to starting your car.

Format

Type your copy. The exception is when you are out on a story and must ad lib your report, using notes.

Double or triple space.

When writing for radio, allow about an inch for each margin. For television, do not use the whole width of the page. Use the right half (or two-thirds, if that your station's preferred format) of the page for your story. The left side of the television script is reserved for video and audio information for the director. This information will indicate a videotape roll, a voice-over (VO), a still store graphic (SS), a Chyron graphic (CHY), or some other visual effect. It also will identify who (on- or off-camera) will be heard.

Type all video and audio information in *capital letters*. In this way, this information is set apart from the words that are read on the air. Because it looks different the chance of a mix-up is reduced. (And anything that reduces the likelihood of a mix-up in broadcasting is a plus.) This is one reason it's a good idea to write news stories in both upper and lower case. Other arguments for using upper and lower case are that we all (newscasters included) are more experienced at reading material printed in upper and lower case, that it enables the newscaster to recognize proper names more readily, and that it is easier to identify the beginnings and endings of sentences.

Make at least one copy of your script. Although computerized newsrooms rely less on multiple copies, some television newsrooms may require as many as seven.

Date the first page of your script. Type your initials (or last name) in the upper left corner of every page.

Use paragraphs. When you start your story *indent*.

In radio, number the pages of your script. Use a separate page for each story or write several short stories on the same page, whichever procedure is followed by your station or network. The advantage of using separate pages is that the order can be changed, and stories can be added or dropped, without marking your script. In computerized newsrooms, of course, such changes can easily be made electronically.

In television, the *stories* are generally numbered. Pages are arranged according to story numbers. And each story is on a separate page. If a story runs more than one page—and this goes for both radio and television—write "MORE" in parentheses at the bottom of the page.

If more than one page is required, end the first page with a *complete* sentence, preferably with a *complete* paragraph. Pages sometimes get out of order, and it is a nightmarish experience, on the air, to turn a page in the middle of a sentence and find the rest of the sentence missing. (It's even worse to find the rest of the story missing!)

If it takes only one more line to complete a story, and you have come to the usual end of a page, don't start another page for just one line. Type it in at the bottom.

Turn in a *clean* script. Retype the story (or re-edit on your terminal) if you have made revisions and time permits. (You will always be fighting the limitations of time.) Newscasters often mark their scripts or do further editing. Their markings, plus yours, can make the final script difficult to read. Professional newswriters pride themselves on clean copy.

Corrections

Making corrections is easy, of course, in computerized newsrooms. When corrections are required, newswriters simply make the corrections electronically on their terminals or computers. They can insert, delete, or change words in a matter of seconds. Then they simply print the corrected version of the story. (Always remember to destroy earlier versions of stories once they have been corrected and printed.)

For those newsrooms still using typewriters, however, making corrections is more complicated. In these newsrooms corrections must be made manually.

If you need to cross out a word, really cross it out. Black it out completely. The last thing the newscasters want is confusion in what they are trying to read.

If you make a correction in spelling, *rewrite the entire word.* If you are using a pencil or ballpoint pen and not a word processor to make your correction, print the corrected word *clearly. Do not* use proofreader's marks to make corrections. The corrections in

Two persos are reported dead(a/in)priv ate plane cash

near waterloo, Iowa

are small help to the newscaster. They may do for a typesetter, but the anchor on the air needs a completely readable script. The sentence should have been corrected to read

persons   in a private   crash
  Two persos are reported dead a in private plane cash

near Waterloo, Iowa.

Notice that in the properly corrected sentence the period was up next to the last word, *Iowa.* In making such corrections, keep punctuation marks and the words they follow together. Again, this reduces confusion. With the word *Waterloo,* it was easier for the writer, and less confusing for the newscaster, to simply superimpose the capital *W.* This kind of minor correcting can be done *only* when it does not make the script more difficult to read.

Do not cross out consecutive words individually. Take the sentence

He will report when they turn in their findings after the first of the year.

Do not edit the sentence so that, in your copy, it looks like this:

He will report ~~when they turn in their findings~~ after the first of the year.

The sentence, if you choose to delete those six words, should look like this:

He will report ~~when they turn in their findings~~ after the first of the year.

Separately crossed-out words in succession tend to confuse. The eye is conditioned to regard such linear units as words.

And here is an example of horrendous "steeplechase" editing from an actual script:

The United States attorney's office ~~said~~ *says* it ~~would~~ *will* not ~~aks~~ *ask* for ~~an~~ a jail sentence.

Such verbal hurdles are inexcusable in a script. In this case, most of the second half of the line should have been crossed out and corrections made like this:

The United States attorney's office ~~said it would~~ *says it will* ~~not ask for an~~ *not ask for* a jail sentence.

Clarity of language—all meaning—is annulled if your corrections of typographical errors or other mistakes cause the newscaster to stumble about in reading the sentence you tried so hard to write simply and well.

Punctuation

Don't overpunctuate. With rare exceptions, the only punctuation marks you need in writing news for broadcast are the period, comma, question mark, and dash.

Forget the semicolon.

In broadcast writing place commas after phrases like "In London," "Here in this country," "At the United Nations," etc., when used at the start of a sentence.

Don't hyphenate at the end of a line if you can help it. Complete words are easier to read.

Regardless of what Webster's says, hyphenate words like *semi-annual, non-fiction, co-defendant,* and *anti-pollution.* By ignoring the dictionary in such cases, you make the words easier to read on the air. The only excuse for punctuation in your script is the help it gives the newscaster in reading, so that the listeners, in turn, can better understand what they hear.

The dash is two hyphens. It is useful for indicating pauses and setting off parenthetical phrases.

Three periods (. . .) can be used in much the same way as the comma. Do *not* use the ellipsis (three periods) in the standard manner—to indicate omitted matter in a quotation. Listeners can't hear the three periods, so they serve no purpose.

In editing quotations, care must be taken not to distort what was said. Repeat: Be careful in editing what a person says. Do not distort.

It is awkward and unnecessary to start and end a quotation with the verbal quotation marks *quote* and *unquote*. Remember, we're trying to write conversationally, and we virtually never hear someone talking that way. Usually a quotation can be adequately identified by such natural attributing phrases as the following:

> He attacked the program, *calling it* "a boondoggle and a sham."

> The mayor was, *in her words*, "full of promises God Almighty cannot redeem."

> The city is, *as she put it*, "just a whisker away from bankruptcy."

> *He put it this way*: "That would be a cold day in hell."

Often newswriters can paraphrase a comment more clearly and succinctly than using a direct quote. If so, you should feel free to use the paraphrase. However, if the quote is distinctive, colorful, dramatic, emotional, or in some other way adds special meaning to the story, then probably you should use it.

Be careful where you place quotation marks, which one broadcaster has described as "those pesky little marks which look so pretty in print but which utter not a sound on the air." If read on the air, this sentence would be confusing:

> The defendant said that, if released on bail, he would go "where I always go."

The listener does not know whether *I* refers to the defendant or to the newscaster. The sentence would be much clearer and more understandable if it read:

> The defendant said that, if released on bail, he would go where he always goes.

Always consider what information a direct quotation adds to your story. What insight does it contribute? Avoid direct quotations that ramble on for three or four sentences. When you use long quotations, it's difficult for the listener to tell where the words of the person being quoted stop and the newscaster's own words begin.

Don't try "personalized" punctuation—i.e., unconventional, ungrammatical punctuation designed to make copy easier to read—unless you're writing for yourself or have had experience writing for the newscaster and *know* how she or he wants it. For example, some newscasters frequently pause before verbs. They believe the sentence sounds better with the pause. But it would be a mistake to sprinkle commas indiscriminately before verbs, since the newscaster who uses this style of reading does not pause before every verb. You—the newswriter—may not be able to sense which pause is right.

Stick to the general, accepted rules for punctuation until you know a newscaster's peculiar needs.

Abbreviations

Most abbreviations should be avoided. As a general rule, words used in broadcast news copy should look the way they are to be read. The rule does not apply to "supers" (titles, place names, and names of organizations) appearing for identification purposes on the TV screen. There isn't room for these to be spelled out.

Names of states are written out in full: *Wisconsin*, not *Wis.*; *New York*, not *N.Y.* The rule also applies to countries. An exception is *U-S*, though *U-S* is used less than *United States* in general conversation and has a stilted sound when used repeatedly in a news broadcast.

Names of the months and days of the week are written out in full: *September*, not *Sept.*; *Friday*, not *Fri.*

Military titles are written out. Never use abbreviations such as *Pvt.*, *Capt.*, or *Gen.* for military ranks. *Pfc.* is an exception, because it frequently is read "P-F-C" instead of "Private First Class."

The abbreviations *Dr.*, *Mr.*, and *Ms.* are fine, but *Prof.* for *Professor* is not encouraged. Avoid such abbreviations as *Dist. Atty.* or *Asst. Dir.*

The abbreviations A.M. and P.M. are permissible, but it is usually more conversational and understandable to refer to times as being "in the morning," "in the afternoon," or "in the evening." Also, it is natural to use time references such as *yesterday afternoon* or *tomorrow morning*. Other time abbreviations, like *E.S.T.* or *C.D.T.*, should be written out.

Abbreviations like *U-N*, *I-O-U*, or *C-N-N* should be hyphenated (not written *UN*, *IOU*, or *CNN*) to tell the newscaster that the separate initials should be read. We, and most stylebooks, recommend hyphens between letters for clarity. In fact, a good rule of thumb is to hyphenate when each initial is to be read separately. It is *not* appropriate to use the hyphen in abbreviations like *NATO*, *NASA*, or *HUD*, which are read as one word.

The commonly recognized name for some organizations is a combination of letters and words. For example, for the National Collegiate Athletic Association, you could write the abbreviation *N-C-double-A*.

Generally the *full name* of an organization—not its initials—should be reported when it is mentioned for the first time. Exceptions are institutions like the *FBI* and the *YMCA*, which practically everyone recognizes by their initials.

Other sets of initials like *U-A-W, A-I-D,* and *F-C-C* should be used *only* after the full names of the organizations—the United Auto Workers, the Agency for International Development, and the Federal Communications Commission—have been given. Such initials may be readily recognizable to you, but many listeners have forgotten, or never knew, which organization or agency names those initials represent.

Numbers

Spell out numbers from one through nine. Use figures for all other numbers, but always write out *thousand, million, billion,* etc. For example, write:

3-million, 8-thousand instead of 3,008,000
8-billion, 600-million instead of 8,600,000,000

Whereas the eye can readily take in (and the mind almost instantly translate) a three-digit number such as 213, the mind finds it more difficult to translate to speech a figure like 3,008,000. You, the writer, translate for the newscaster—and for yourself when you are the reporter—by writing *3-million, 8-thousand.*

Round off large numbers. For example, if the allocation for a federal project is $6,512,000, you can say that the allocation is "six and a half million dollars." The listener assumes that you are not reporting the amount down to the last dollar and cent. If you want to be more precise, you can say that the allocation amounts to "a little more than six and a half million dollars."

Never write the figure as "$6.5 million." It's not much better to write the figure as "6-point-5-million dollars." Why not say "six-and-a-half million dollars" as people usually do in conversation?

When writing for broadcast, it is easy to use too many numbers and to use numbers that are too complicated. Don't write, as one newspaper correspondent did:

After four straight losing sessions, stocks recovered Tuesday as investors entered the market pushing the Dow Jones Industrial Average up 15.87 to 3,230.90 on volume of 194.53 million shares, up nearly 34 million shares from the 160.62 million shares traded during the previous session.

This detailed information is useful and the newspaper reader can digest it—that's an advantage of the print media over radio and television. In newscasts so many figures in such a short time become an audio blur to the audience. The broadcast version of the story should read something like this:

Stocks bounced back today, recovering some of the losses of the past four sessions. The Dow Jones Industrial Average was up almost 16 points, closing at 32-31. About 200 million shares were traded.

This business of rounding off and translating figures in the interest of making stories less complicated, and hence more understandable, *can* be carried too far. For example, it would be absurd to say 100 people died in an airplane crash when 103 died. But it would be preferable to report that the crash occurred about 100 miles north of Dallas rather than 106 miles. In this story the exact distance does not really matter.

Incidentally, most stylebooks say that usage of *one thousand, one million,* etc., is preferable to *a thousand, a million,* etc. The reasoning is that *a thousand* may sound like *eight thousand* to a listener. Although this may be, we know of no actual cases where this has created a problem, and because *a thousand* is more conversational, we are going along with that style.

Sometimes distances—inches, feet, and yards—can be roughly translated to make a smaller figure. Thus, thirty-six inches can be referred to as "three feet," or "a yard," and five thousand feet as "nearly a mile."

Fractions are always written out: *one-half, two-thirds,* etc. Fractions can be used to simplify—again by translating. "One-third of the money will go for housing" is better broadcast copy than "Thirty percent of the money will go for housing." And isn't it easier to say (and to understand) "Food prices have almost doubled," than "Food prices have risen 95 percent?"

One last word about numbers: the fewer you throw at listeners, the more understandable you are. Always keep in mind that listeners cannot read the numbers, yet they have to remember them. And they have to remember, at the same time, what you said about them. So when you are thinking of using a figure—any figure—think twice. Ask yourself if it is necessary. If it *is* necessary, give it to the listener in its simplest form.

Dates

In writing the day of the month, follow the standard rules for numbers and add the *st, nd, rd,* or *th* that we normally use in conversation. For example, make it "May 16th," not "May 16;" "January first," not "January 1;" and "October 21st," not "October 21."

Symbols

Don't use them. Symbols such as $, %, and # are anathema to the newscaster and will not be suffered. Instead, use *dollar, percent,* and *number.* Also avoid *No.,* as in *"No. 66."* Write out "Number 66."

Celsius and Fahrenheit

In weather stories some broadcasters use *Celsius* as well as *Fahrenheit* in reporting temperatures. If the metric system ever becomes popular in this country, you may be giving temperatures only in terms of the centigrade (Celsius) scale. Zero is the Celsius temperature at which water freezes, and 100 is the temperature at which it boils. The respective temperatures on the Fahrenheit scale, which is still in common use in this country, are 32 and 212 degrees.

Active Voice

Broadcast newswriters should use verbs in the active voice whenever possible. This is one of the basic principles in writing broadcast news. "A car hit him" is much more direct and forthright than "He was hit by a car." In comparison, the passive voice is weak and unconversational. Remember always the importance of *active voice*.

Grammar

One of the most frequent complaints news directors have about their writers is that they are ignorant of English grammar. Even though the writers probably studied—and often mastered—basic grammatical principles in college, they often have difficulty translating their grammatical knowledge into the practice of broadcast newswriting.

Instruction in English grammar is beyond the province of this text. If you have trouble with grammar, you should work on improving it. The library or any good bookstore can provide you what you always wanted to know about grammar.

Two excellent, understandable texts on the subject are R. Thomas Berner's *Language Skills for Journalists,* published by Houghton Mifflin, and *Working with Words: A Concise Guide for Media Editors and Writers,* by Brian S. Brooks and James L. Pinson, published by St. Martin's Press. Also, William Zinsser's *On Writing Well,* from Harper & Row, may be the best book of essays on the subject since E. B. White updated William Strunk's classic *Elements of Style,* published by Macmillan. Both are enthusiastically recommended.

Grammar, the rules for use of language, IS important.

3. *Names and Pronunciation*

In any reporting, the most important thing about names is to get them right, but in broadcasting names are treated differently than in other media—they are simplified wherever possible. When identification does not suffer for it, first names and initials are left out. The broadcaster says "President Clinton" and "Secretary of State Christopher," or just "Secretary Christopher" if the name appears in a context that leaves no doubt you are talking about the secretary of state. The broadcaster never has to say "Secretary of State Warren Christopher."

This is consistent with the guiding principle in writing news for radio and television, which is to tell your story as effectively as possible in the fewest number of words. Through simplification you improve communication between yourself and the person listening. The listener's mind isn't being cluttered with nonessential information. The "shape" of your message has cleaner lines.

In local news the first names of mayors may be omitted. In New York City, for example, local newscasters refer to "Mayor Giuliani," not "Mayor Rudolph Giuliani." Include the first name, however, if the mayor holds office in a city other than your own.

In national stories first names and initials can most often be dropped from the names of governors and members of Congress. For example:

Governor Allen of Virginia
Senator Kerry of Massachusetts
Representative Mickel of Illinois

Now it gets a little more complicated. When the politician's party affiliation is important to the story, this style usually is used:

Republican Governor Allen of Virginia
Democratic Senator Kerry of Massachusetts
Republican Representative Michel of Illinois

This is better broadcast style than

Governor Allen, Republican of Virginia
Senator Kerry, Democrat of Massachusetts
Representative Mickel, Republican of Illinois

and *much* better than

Virginia Republican Governor George F. Allen of Virginia
Massachusetts Democratic Senator John F. Kerry
Illinois Republican Representative Robert H. Michel.

"Freight train" phrases like these are abhorred, and those who perpetrate them deserve to read their own words.

When a member of Congress chairs a committee, the position may be more significant than the fact that he or she is a senator or representative. Then that person need not be identified as senator or representative. Thus, instead of "Senator Byrd, chairman of the Senate Appropriations Committee," it's better to say "Chairman Byrd of the Senate Appropriations Committee." The redundancy of using both *senator* and *Senate* is avoided.

Remember, these are guidelines. None of this means you should never use the first names of members of Congress. It means you can usually leave them out. By leaving them out, you make a less complicated sentence. But there is nothing wrong, for example, with "The chairman of the House Ways and Means Committee, Dan Rostenkowski, said today he strongly disagrees," although "Chairman Rostenkowski of the House Ways and Means Committee said today he strongly disagrees," says the same thing and saves two words.

Do not identify senators as *congressmen* or *congresswomen*. The terms are synonyms for *representative*. Reserve them for members of the House of Representatives.

It is a habit picked up from newspapers to write names like Edwin "Buzz" Armstrong or Edmund "Jerry" Brown. Choose. Call these people by their nickname or their first name, not both. Use one or the other as you would in conversation. But be sensitive to usage, lest you appear biased. It's one thing to say Jerry Brown, the name most commonly used, and another to speak of the senior senator from Massachusetts as Teddy Kennedy.

In the boycotting of initials, note two exceptions. Use the initial with common surnames like Smith and Jones, especially if crime is involved. In a local newscast, the person's address provides further protection against misidentification and possible libel. Also use the initial in names like George M. Cohan, Edward R. Murrow, D. W. Griffith, and George C. Scott. In a sense, the initials are their trademark.

More About Names

It is permissible to start a news story with a well-known name—"Frank Sinatra made a surprise appearance on Capitol Hill today"—but *never* start with an unfamiliar name. Listeners will, for the moment, be baffled. Because the name is strange to them, they have to be prepared for it. "Preparation" consists of reporting the person's occupation, function, title—whatever serves to identify—*first* and name *second*. Don't write "Keith Brodie, president of Duke University, announced today that he plans to resign." Instead, write "The president of Duke University, Keith Brodie, announced today that he plans to resign." The name is now "teed up." When listeners hear the words "president of Duke University," they expect to hear a name, and now the name has meaning.

It is especially important in the treatment of names to remember that you are writing for the ear. (That phrase again.) Unlike newspaper readers, listeners cannot dwell on a name. They hear a surname—sometimes for the fraction of a second— and it is gone. So, never give a person's name in the lead of a story and thereafter keep referring to that person as "he" or "she." Repeat the name. Failure to do so is one of the most aggravating "sins of omission" in broadcast journalism.

Similarly, do not refer in your copy to "the former" or "the latter." This is a carryover from print journalism, where the reader can look back. It imposes on listeners, who cannot look back, an unreasonable obligation to remember and translate. You must give listeners what John Chancellor has aptly described as "understandable information."

And don't bother with names of no significance to the listener. If the governor of a Philippine island appeals for emergency aid after a typhoon, just say the governor made the appeal. Not only might the broadcaster have difficulty pronouncing the governor's name, but the name also contributes nothing to an understanding of what happened. Indeed, it can distract. A pretty good rule is to report names that listeners recognize or will come to recognize because of subsequent events. In short, names that mean something to the listener.

KIGH-roh Is the One in Egypt

This heading is stolen from the *New York Times,* which did an article on the trouble newscasters have with pronunciation. The article observed, among other things, that if a newscaster confuses "KIGH-roh" in Egypt with "KAY-roh" in Illinois, "a certain amount of precious credibility goes out the window."

Mispronunciation does damage credibility, and broadcasters know it. The well-worn dictionaries in station libraries are used more for pronunciation than for spelling. Network newsrooms and some stations have pronunciation guides in their computer systems. These have an advantage over the early handbooks prepared by CBS and NBC in that they can be constantly updated. For more than thirty years CBS enjoyed the services of Dr. Cabell Greet, a professor of speech at Columbia University, as its special consultant on pronunciation. It is due to the instruction of Professor Greet that on CBS you hear *junta* pronounced "JUN-ta." Until he intervened, most broadcasters had given it the Spanish pronunciation, "HOON-ta." He reasoned that since *junta,* pronounced "JUN-ta," had been in English usage since 1623, it should be spoken that way. In his research he found that the Spanish pronunciation was not introduced in the United States until after 1898, when it was brought back by soldiers who had served in Cuba during the Spanish-American War.

For years the BBC employed an advisory committee on spoken English. Its first chairman was a poet laureate of England, Robert Bridges, who said, "We are daily establishing in the minds of the public what correct speech should be." But a later chairman, George Bernard Shaw, called the committee a ghastly failure. "It should be reconstituted," he said, "with an age limit of thirty and a few taxi drivers on it." This from the creator of Professor Higgins, the most celebrated phonetician of them all!

Experts on the pronunciation of certain words are not hard to find—*if* you look in the right place. When the first bulletins identifying Robert Kennedy's assassin were read, you could hear Sirhan Sirhan's name pronounced a dozen different ways. No authority seemed to know the correct pronunciation. Then someone thought to ask the defendant's mother. Why, yes, she said, the name is pronounced "sir-han" rhyming with *pan.* CBS had been pronouncing it "seer-hahn." NBC's pronunciation had been "SEER-hahn." ABC hadn't committed itself. Other ways you may have heard the name that day include "sir-HAN," "sir-HAHN," "SEER-han," "seer-HAHN" and "SIR-AHN!"

Of course, the best source is your dictionary, with its pronunciations of the names of people and places. Unabridged dictionaries are especially good in this respect. But many names are not to be found readily in print. What do you do then?

There are various things you can do. If you don't know the pronunciation of the name of an official of a foreign country, or how to pronounce the name of one of its towns or provinces, call the consulate of that country. If you're in Washington, call the embassy. New York stations often are helped in their pronunciation problems by the United Nations. If it's the name of a politician, call the politician's office or the local political organization. If it's the name of a labor leader, call union headquarters. If it's a member of an African American organization, try the organization.

Be resourceful. On occasion, when we were desperate for the pronunciation for a seldom-heard-of-town, we turned to "Ma Bell." We simply called the telephone operator in that community. We'd ask, "How do you pronounce the name of your town?'' Sounds crazy, but it cost little and it worked. One of us boasted that from his desk in New York he got the correct pronunciation for Elizabethton, Tennessee, in fifteen seconds. (It's ''E-liz-a-BETH-ton''.)

The best advice on pronunciation is: do not assume you know. In 1992 charges of sexual harassment abounded in the news. Day after day anchors, network and local, mispronounced *harassment*. They stressed the second syllable, so it came out ''har-ASS-ment.'' They did this because the verb is pronounced ''har-ASS.'' They assumed consistency. The correct pronunciation is HAR-ass-ment.

Bill Monroe, who had a distinguished career at NBC, likes to tell the story about an announcer's mispronunciation of the name of Fred Preaus, a Louisiana politician. The announcer snatched a piece of copy from the AP broadcast wire and, reading it word for word on the air—with total disregard for what he was saying—declared pontifically, ''Fred Preaus, whose name rhymes with moose, today announced his candidacy for governor.'' Besides reading aloud the AP advisory on pronunciation, which he was not supposed to do, the announcer had compounded his mistake by giving *Preaus* the French pronunciation ''Pro.'' He assumed this was right because the name is French. A lot of listeners, hearing the reference to *moose,* must have done a double-take.

There is a real lesson here. If you are reading, don't pontificate. If you stumble in your arrogance, you fall farther, and harder, because you are revealed as a fake. And *don't* assume.

Know What You Are Reading

In pronouncing place names, never trust the way a word looks. For example, *Pago Pago* is pronounced ''PANG-o PANG-o.'' (A student intern at a station in Washington, D.C., won a five-dollar bet on that one!) Within a matter of minutes a network correspondent who should know better was heard pronouncing *Edinburgh* as though it rhymed with *Pittsburgh* and *Gloucester,* the Massachusetts fishing port, ''GLOW-ster'' instead of ''GLOSS-ter.'' Such mispronunciations do cause listeners to wonder if the newscaster is well informed. They damage credibility.

There is an inconsistency in the pronunciation of place names. *Miami,* for example, frequently is pronounced ''my-AM-a,'' not ''my-AM-ee,'' by people living in Miami, and citizens of Cincinnati often say ''sin-sa-NAT-a,'' instead of ''sin-sa-NAT-ee.'' Likewise, *St. Louis* sometimes is pronounced ''saint-LOO-ee,'' as in the song ''St. Louis Blues.'' The generally accepted pronunciations for the three cities are ''my-AM-ee,'' ''sin-sa-NAT-ee'' and ''saint-LOO-iss.'' Visitors to New York City often pronounce *Houston* Street like the city in Texas. But it's pronounced ''HOWS-ton.''

We began this section by noting the difference between ''KIGH-roh,'' Egypt, and ''KAY-roh,'' Illinois. Other look-alikes pronounced differently are:

BO-fort, N.C. and *BU-fert*, S.C. (Beaufort)
BURR-lin, N.H. and *Burr-LIN*, Germany (Berlin)
Cal-las, Maine and *Cal-aye*, France (Calais)
CAN-ton, Ohio and *Can-TAWN*, China (Canton, now called Guangzhou.)
KWIN-see, Illinois and *KWIN-zee*, Mass. (Quincy)
LYE-ma, Ohio and *LEE-ma*, Peru (Lima)
MY-lan, Ohio and *Me-LAHN*, Italy (Milan)
Moss-cow, N.Y. and *MOSS-co*, Russia (Moscow)
NEW-erk, N.J. and *NEW-ark*, Del. (Newark)

There are instances when an uncommon, though correct, pronunciation strikes the listener as an affectation. Few American newscasters, for example, have—or in most cases should have—the temerity to pronounce *either* as "EYE-ther." As Fowler says in the preface to his *Modern English Usage*, "Display of superior knowledge is as great a vulgarity as display of superior wealth."

Don't ignore listeners' critiques on pronunciation. They're often right!

In many newsrooms it is the writer's responsibility to check pronunciations for the newscaster. If you are the reporter doing the story, obviously *you* need to know. This information—the correct pronunciation of a word—should be typed in *capital letters,* within parentheses, either above or immediately after the word in question. For examples:

(EK-O-LOGICAL)
They discussed the ecological aspects of the problem.
Ecology (EE-KOL-OGY) was the major subject discussed.

The pronunciations are rendered in capital letters to set them apart.

The broadcast wires operated by the Associated Press and United Press International have adopted a system of phonetic spelling for hard-to-pronounce names—they cannot transmit the pronunciation symbols used by biographical dictionaries and gazetteers. These phonetic spellings provided by the wire services are given in parentheses after the names, not above them, for obvious reasons. They are provided *only* on the broadcast wires.

Correspondents traveling to Concord, New Hampshire, for the quadrennial primary should know by now that Concord is pronounced "KON-kerd," not "Konkord." And possibly the most frequently mispronounced words in broadcast news are *prepare*, *prevent*, and *provide*. Take a close look. Their first syllables are *pre* and *pro*. They should be pronounced "pre-PARE," "pre-VENT," and pro-VIDE." But what is heard too often is "PURR-pare," "PURR-vent," and "PURR-vide."

Pronunciation is serious business. It is bad enough not to know how to pronounce a foreign name, but to be ignorant—and there is no kinder word for it—of how to pronounce a good American word is embarrassing for all concerned. As Allan Jackson of CBS said in one of his broadcast journalism lectures, ''Nothing is quite so distracting to a listener as a news broadcaster who can't pronounce the words of his own language.''

The actor David Garrick said of preacher George Whitefield (''WHIT-field''), ''He could make men laugh or cry by pronouncing the word *Mesopotamia*.'' Many a writer could weep over the pronunciation a newscaster gave a word selected oh-so-carefully. And many a listener, hearing that word, has laughed.

If you are a staff writer, do not assume that because the person you write for is intelligent and well traveled, he or she knows. Make certain. Then there will be no need to laugh *or* weep.

You have now come to Chapter 4. In the first three chapters you discovered that broadcast newswriting has a history. You have seen some of the work of those who excelled in writing news for broadcast, and because the work of such writers is instructive, you will see more.

You have been reminded of the importance of pronunciation and been shown the best way to handle abbreviations, numbers, dates, and names. The rules are elementary. They are not arbitrary. They evolved from the experience of radio and TV journalists over many years. They make your script more readable and what you read more understandable, which is what communication is about.

So much for ''rules.''

4. Tell *Your Story*

The time: Seconds before 5:47 P.M., April 12, 1945.
The place: New York City

Editors on the second floor of the Times Building discuss their lead story: three United States armies—the 1st, 3rd, and 9th—are pressing toward Berlin. Armored elements of the 9th Army have crossed the Elbe River in force. Also on Page One will appear the report of new air strikes against American warships off Okinawa. The U.S. Navy has lost a destroyer and the Japanese have lost 118 planes.

Across town, on the seventeenth floor of the CBS Building, John Daly is writing his evening newscast. He is due to go on the air at 6:15. The news he intends to report has, basically, the same portent as that which is being set in type at the *New York Times*. Victory in Europe is imminent. More hard fighting appears inevitable in the Pacific.

In those few seconds an era ends. At 5:47 P.M. bells begin jangling on the International News Service teletype at both the *Times* and CBS, and in all newsrooms that subscribe to INS. CBS World News Editor Lee Otis walks quickly to the teletype and reads the flash: FDR DEAD. Two minutes later—at 5:49 P.M.—CBS engineers have interrupted the radio serial "Wilderness Road," and Daly, at the microphone in Studio Nine, is saying

We interrupt this program to bring you a special news bulletin from CBS World News. A press association has just announced that President Roosevelt is dead. All that has been received is that bare announcement. There are no further details as yet, but CBS World News will return to the air in just a few moments with more information as it is received in

our New York headquarters. We return you now to our regularly scheduled program.

Let's look a little more closely and critically at this historic bulletin.

First, the news that President Roosevelt had died should have been repeated at
least once. Of the five sentences in the bulletin, only one refers directly to the death
of the president of the United States. The source of this unexpected news should
have been clearly identified as the International News Service. And press associations
don't ''announce'' the death of presidents; they ''report'' it. Furthermore, it is surprising that after receiving this news the network rejoined its regularly scheduled
program, even for a few moments. That would not happen today. As they did when
President Kennedy was shot, all networks would start giving continuous coverage.

As it was, within two minutes after reading his bulletin, Daly was back on the
air, reporting the cause of death—cerebral hemorrhage—and plans for the funeral:

Funeral services will be held Saturday afternoon in the East Room of the
White House. Interment will be at Hyde Park.

Through the night, coverage of the death of the president continued on CBS and
other radio networks. It was the first death of an incumbent president to be covered
by journalists of the new medium. Eighteen years would pass before a comparable
tragedy would again challenge broadcast journalists' technical and reportorial skills.

At the *New York Times*, reporters, editors, and printers grappled with their biggest
story since D-day. Obviously, the original front-page dummy was scrapped. The
American advance on Berlin became the number two story. The headline across the
top of the page now read

PRESIDENT ROOSEVELT IS DEAD;
    TRUMAN TO CONTINUE POLICIES;
        9TH CROSSES ELBE, NEARS BERLIN

Arthur Krock, chief Washington correspondent, wrote the lead story.

WASHINGTON, April 12—Franklin Delano Roosevelt, President of
the United States and the only Chief Executive in history who was chosen
for more than two terms, died suddenly and unexpectedly at 4:35 o'clock
P.M. today at Warm Springs, Ga., and the White House announced his
death at 5:14 o'clock. He was 63.

This initial coverage by CBS and the *Times* can be compared in many ways: speed
of communication, depth of coverage, and audience. But let's look at another aspect:
the language used by the two media, the differences in reportorial style.

John Daly was *telling* what happened.

A press association has just announced that President Roosevelt is dead. . . . Funeral services will be held Saturday afternoon in the East Room of the White House.

This is how people talk. "I just heard Mrs. Smith died. The funeral will be Friday afternoon at the church." The style is conversational. It is natural. It is right.

In broadcasting the first bulletin, all Daly had before him was a slip of yellow paper from the INS machine bearing two words: "FDR DEAD." Later he adlibbed from wire copy from all three wire services—AP and UP, as well as INS—before switching to Washington for firsthand reports. Daly said

He had gone to Warm Springs to try to get new strength to face the San Francisco Conference, to shape there with his own hands, as much as he could, the course of the peace to come, to lead there men of all nations and all faiths, to sit down together around the council table and to give the gift that he had always wanted—the gift of peace that would last beyond our time, perhaps beyond our children's time, and to the time of our grandchildren.

That is an extraordinarily long sentence—eighty-seven words—much too long according to every style book that has been written for broadcast news. But it flows. It is conversational, albeit in Daly's individual, rather ornate style. And because it is beautifully structured—full of pauses—it is completely understandable. It is also eloquent.

Compare the broadcast language of John Daly with the print language of Arthur Krock. To the ear alone—without sight—Krock's language is insufferable. He begins with the name of the president and then spends the next nineteen words identifying him. You are deep in the sentence before you are told that the president died. The sentence would confuse listeners with its conglomeration of facts and figures: "Franklin Delano Roosevelt . . . only Chief Executive . . . history . . . two terms . . . died . . . 4:35 o'clock P.M. . . . Warm Springs . . . White House . . . 5:14 o'clock"— all in one sentence. Also, phrases are used that practically no one uses in conversation: "4:35 o'clock P.M." and "5:14 o'clock." You just don't talk that way. Imagine a friend saying "I'll meet you in the lobby at 8 o'clock P.M."! Krock's next sentence, "He was 63," is ideal broadcast copy, but the number follows on the heels of 4:35 and 5:14—not the kind of thing you want to do in writing for radio or television.

One reason Daly could deliver an eighty-seven-word sentence and not confuse the listener is that he was emphasizing *one idea*—Roosevelt's desire to do what he could to make a lasting peace. One idea to a sentence is an excellent guide. Krock's lead held a devastating assortment.

So here are four important differences between writing news for broadcast and writing for print.

1. Broadcast news is telling—not chronicling—what happened. The style should be conversational and informal, but not too cozy.
2. No array of facts—especially figures—should be thrown at the listener or viewer all at once. The fewer figures the better.
3. Each sentence, ideally, should contain only one idea or image.
4. Generally, sentences should be brief.

Ernest Hemingway was quoted as saying "Good writing is good conversation, only more so." Nowhere is this more true than in broadcast journalism. In this case the "more so" means that writers of news for radio and television must be more selective in what they talk about, and in the way they say it, than they might be while chatting with friends. But, to be good, their writing will have to be conversational.

Many broadcast news writers have been told that they should write as though they were talking to the person "at the next bar stool." Although this familiar adage overstates the case a bit, the point is correct. The best test of broadcast newswriting is whether it sounds as you would sound when talking informally to a friend.

To write conversationally has implications beyond story focus, word choice, and sentence length. It describes an overall approach in which newswriters see themselves as telling stories, not just stringing together facts or writing words. Just as news anchors are often criticized for "reading words" rather than telling stories, newswriters are well advised to think in terms of the overall stories they are telling.

If someone asks you what you did today, you don't first describe how you woke up, then chronologically recite every event that occurred. In answering the question, you would typically select one or two highlights of your day and describe them with appropriate detail. The broadcast newswriter's strategy is the same. The facts, the meat of the story, are essential. But what distinguishes good broadcast news writing is the way in which those facts are used to *tell a story*.

The Enemy is Confusion

Just as the person who writes science articles for a popular magazine must be able to translate complicated scientific data into everyday language, the writer of broadcast news must make complicated stories sound simple without demeaning them. Few listeners, for example, have the background necessary to understand the workings of the Common Market. A story concerning the market must be written in such a way as to be universally meaningful—that is, meaningful to the mechanic in Omaha as well as the economist at Stanford.

More than two centuries ago Daniel Defoe said, "If any man were to ask me what I would suppose to be a perfect style of language, I would answer that in which a man speaking to five hundred people all of common and various capacities should be understood by them all." Instead of writing to be understood by five hundred people, "all of common and various capacities," broadcast journalists may be writing for five million. They must sort out the facts—the essential from the nonessential. Then they must make the essential understandable. They must translate.

Take the quotation from Defoe. The idea expressed is excellent. But for radio or television Defoe's style is horrendous. Even in print you may need to read the sentence twice to capture its meaning.

In broadcasting, understanding must be immediate. It is of no value that your facts are straight, your copy is clean, and your grammar is faultless *if* your listeners make no sense out of what they hear. In writing news for the ear, the "perfect style of language" is that which makes your meaning—what you are reporting—clear to a harassed motorist in rush-hour traffic and to a person trying to prepare dinner in a busy household.

There are many requirements for good style, but in writing news for broadcast the first requirement is clarity. Not just clarity for listeners with college degrees but clarity for people of "various capacities." Remembering the rule "Never underestimate the listener's intelligence or overestimate his or her knowledge," you write "down" to no one. But the language must be universal. You are writing for all manner of people who depend on you to be informed.

You must remember that your listener has only one chance to hear, and understand, your news story. Newspaper readers can reread a sentence, a paragraph, or a whole story if they don't understand it at first. Radio listeners and television viewers don't have that luxury. They have to understand it the first time around. They have "only one chance." As a broadcast journalist it makes no difference how good you are or how important is what you want to say is, if you are not understood.

The Challenge

A 240-word story moves on the AP newspaper wire. Your newscast is tight, without much room for additional copy. The producer tells you to boil the story down to fifteen seconds. In other words, reduce the 240 words to about 40 words. Here is the story, in most of its original form, as it moved on AP June 17, 1992.

WASHINGTON (AP)—PROFITS AT THE NATION'S SAVINGS AND LOANS REBOUNDED IN THE FIRST THREE MONTHS OF 1992 TO $1.59 BILLION, THE BEST PERFORMANCE FOR THE TROUBLED INDUSTRY IN SIX YEARS, THE GOVERNMENT SAID WEDNESDAY.

EARNINGS AT THE 2,064 INSTITUTIONS THAT HAVE ESCAPED SEIZURE BY THE GOVERNMENT MORE THAN DOUBLED FROM $610 MILLION A YEAR AGO, THE OFFICE OF THRIFT SUPERVISION SAID.

IT WAS THE FIFTH STRAIGHT QUARTERLY PROFIT, THE OFFICE SAID, WITH 93 PERCENT OF THE INSTITUTIONS REPORTING EARNINGS.

AND WITH THE TAKEOVER OF 711 S&Ls SINCE 1989, ONLY 37 S&Ls REMAIN ON THE AGENCY'S EXPECTED-TO-FAIL LIST.

"THE END OF THE CLEANUP . . . IS IN SIGHT," TIMOTHY RYAN, THRIFT OFFICE DIRECTOR, TOLD THE SENATE BANKING COMMITTEE TODAY.

HOWEVER, THE CONGRESSIONAL BUDGET OFFICE AND PRIVATE ANALYSTS OFFERED LAWMAKERS A LESS ROSY VIEW.

AS MANY AS 650 S&Ls MAY YET FAIL, SAID ROBERT REISCHAUER, BUDGET OFFICE DIRECTOR, ADDING THAT MANY EXPERTS BELIEVE THE INDUSTRY CANNOT BE DECLARED FULLY HEALTHY UNTIL REAL ESTATE MARKETS RECOVER.

"THE CLEANUP OF THE THRIFT CRISIS IS NOT OVER," REISCHAUER TOLD THE COMMITTEE. . . . THRIFTS ARE STILL NOT AS PROFITABLE AS THEY ONCE WERE."

HOWEVER, HE CONCEDED THAT THE INDUSTRY DATA "PROVIDE ROOM FOR GUARDED OPTIMISM ABOUT ITS LONG-TERM VIABILITY, ALBEIT AS A MUCH SMALLER PLAYER."

THE TWO KEY REASONS FOR THE RECENT IMPROVEMENT, THE THRIFT OFFICE SAID, ARE THE GOVERNMENT SEIZURES OF INSOLVENT S&Ls SINCE 1989 AND THE MOST FAVORABLE INTEREST RATE CONDITIONS FOR FINANCIAL INSTITUTIONS SINCE THE 1970s.

Here is what a writer at an all-news radio station, faced with the challenge, did with the story.

The government says the Savings and Loan industry is more profitable than it has been for six years. But despite profits of one-point-six billion dollars for the first three months of 1992, the Congressional Budget Office says don't be too optimistic . . . that as many as 650 more Savings and Loans may fail.

In taking less than one-tenth the time to tell the story, the writer has omitted a great deal of detail. It is the kind of compression of news that leads to the description of broadcast journalism as a "headline service." This is warranted to some degree—the public should not rely solely on radio and television news reports—but longer stories *are* carried by all networks and many stations.

The writer reported the heart of the story, avoiding long and confusing phrases like "guarded optimism about its long-term viability" and "the fact that 90 percent of the industry is doing well is secondary to how the worst 5 or 10 percent are doing because that's where the threat lies." The story is in plain-spoken English. And, one might add, it is easily read and understood.

Here is what veteran correspondent John Hart did with a long wire service story, turning it into a small masterpiece:

In Northern Ireland, a 17-year-old girl was cut by men wearing hoods and carrying razors. She's Catholic. Her boy friend is Protestant. She's alive, and she has a cross carved in her forehead.

It's not how many words you have that matters.

Contractions

Contractions are common in conversation, but the person starting out to write news for broadcast seems instinctively to avoid them. If you read your script out loud, you should quickly notice the difference between the awkward and stilted ''He did not say whether he will run for the school board . . .'' and the more conversational ''He didn't say whether he'll run for. . . .''

Notice how often we use contractions when we talk. The examples are everywhere: ''The employees aren't eligible . . .'' or ''There's no question it was an important vote.''

There are times to contract and times not to contract, and usually the choice is determined by an instinctive feeling as to which is preferable. The contraction is definitely less formal—more casual as well as more conversational. Contractions generally aren't quite as strong—*don't* is not as forceful as *do not*. Because contractions are more informal, they might not be appropriate in a serious story. You would be more likely to say ''That is the latest death toll . . .'' than ''That's the latest death toll. . . .'' There is no rule for this. You have to feel it. It can be generalized, however, that contractions are used much more freely in broadcast journalism than in the print media.

Be Certain

Because of the ephemeral nature of radio and television, they are more likely than newspapers to be misunderstood. The newscaster's words are fleeting; the picture is evanescent—now you see it and now you don't. This transitory quality affects—*should* affect—how you write. Extra effort must be made to avoid confusion in what you say and what you show. Meaning must be clearly established because, as said earlier, neither listeners nor viewers can play back what they have just heard or seen.

In a sense, radio and television news writers sometimes provide ''playbacks'' for their audiences. On occasion, to remove doubt, they will repeat a crucial number, name, phrase, or even a whole sentence so the listener may be sure what was said. Remember the FDR bulletin example presented at the beginning of this chapter. We said John Daly should have repeated the information at least once. Repetition is good practice whenever a fact needs underscoring: for example, the description of a fugitive bank robber or the telephone number to call for information in an emergency.

A fact likely to be missed by listeners is the location of a news event. They hear that an explosion has occurred, killing many persons, but some may not have been listening closely until they realized the serious nature of the story. Now, as the newscaster reads, they listen for clues to *where it happened*. But the newscaster never repeats the location, and frustrated listeners scan for other newscasts or wait for the morning paper. Some stations have a rule that the location of the event must be restated somewhere, somehow, toward the bottom of the story.

In obituaries, the name of the deceased should be repeated. Remember your own frustration when, having missed the name of someone who died, all you hear are references to *he, she, him,* or *her.*

An obituary for a newscast is written quite differently than one for a newspaper. On January 29, 1993, this obituary appeared in the *Washington Post:*

> Edward P. Morgan, 82, the veteran broadcast journalist and writer who reported for ABC, CBS and the forerunner of the Public Broadcasting Service, died of cancer Jan. 27 at his home in McLean.

That's right for print, wrong for radio and television. The sentence, besides being too long for a newscast, is overloaded with information. It's hard to imagine anyone upon one reading—and there's only one—taking it all in. For broadcast, the sentence might be restructured like this:

> One of the early broadcast journalists, Edward P. Morgan, has died. In his long career, Morgan worked as a reporter and commentator for ABC, CBS and the Public Broadcast Laboratory, which was a forerunner of P-B-S, the Public Broadcasting Service. He died of cancer at his home in McLean, Virginia. Edward P. Morgan was 82.

Note that the broadcast version does not lead with the name. Although Edward P. Morgan was one of broadcasting's most respected journalists, the name was not sufficiently recognizable at the time of his death. Also note that the name is repeated at the end of the story.

In television, obituaries for well-known people often are accompanied by footage illustrating their careers. When Lillian Gish died it was a rare television station that did not show the legendary actress in one of her early films.

"We Interrupt This Program . . ."

Because of the time element—generally commercial time—wordiness, as we have said, is a crime. But if it ever becomes a choice between more words and confusion as to meaning, use more words. Clarity has top priority.

This is especially true of bulletins, which often catch listeners off guard. Example: If an airliner crashes, *repeat* the name of the airline (though the public relations people at the airline may not appreciate that), the flight number, and the place of departure and destination. These facts are essential. If your bulletin is being carried on a major station or network, it's a good bet that many who hear it will, at that very moment, know of some friend or relative who is traveling by air. This procedure should be followed when reporting any sudden tragedy involving mass transportation. The repetition of information is both good reporting and humane behavior.

Sometimes a story is so big the newscaster cannot wait for details, important though they may be. If an airliner explodes in midair after take-off, and the airline to which it belongs is not immediately known, certainly the accident should be reported. But the incompleteness of the report must be emphasized, and the sources of information must be given. And that first bulletin *must* be followed as soon as possible by another bulletin clearly identifying the plane that exploded. Any inaccuracies in the first report *must* be corrected. The broadcast of erroneous, fragmentary information of tragic proportions is as irresponsible as it is cruel.

5. *Watch That Word!*

Eric Sevareid said, "One good word is worth a thousand pictures." In the realm of ideas, words rightly used communicate in a way that is unsurpassed. Think of John Donne's "never send to know for whom the bell tolls," or William Faulkner's creed for writers delivered when he received the Nobel Prize, or Ed Murrow's declaration on the freedom to dissent. Think of the power of words. Ptahhotep said it well in 3400 B.C.: "Be a craftsman in speech, that thou mayest be strong. For the strength of one is the tongue, and speech is mightier than all fighting." This is not to disparage videotape or film, both of which show what is happening. A picture can work miracles in provoking thought. But the word remains man's best tool for the expression of thought. It is the supreme implement.

This chapter provides some tips on how that implement can be used more effectively—and how some pitfalls can be avoided—by the writer of radio and television news.

More Than a Matter of Four-Letter Words

We come to the matter of taste. This is not a matter of eschewing four-letter words; they're still out—at least at this writing. Other judgments are more difficult to make. The boundary between good reporting and bad taste often is poorly defined. For example, in reporting the mutilation of a murder victim, what language do you use? If the murderer obviously was a sexual pervert, how far should you go in reporting the grisly details? Do you imply the nature of the crime by simply saying that the body was mutilated?

Taste changes in radio and television reporting as in everything else. In the 1940s a woman was not raped; she was assaulted or attacked. In most cases the verb was preceded by the adverb *criminally*. (Was such an act ever committed legally?) Networks rarely reported any crime unless it involved well-known figures, famous or infamous, or was committed under bizarre circumstances. Even local stations carried a fraction of the crime news they do today.

The subject of venereal disease was taboo. NBC did not permit use of the word *diaper* on the air until 1947, and then only in comedy "for purposes of dry humor." Coincidentally, the network for the first time approved the singing of the lyrics to the torch ballad "Body and Soul." In his *News on the Air,* Paul White told of a murdered woman in whose brassiere police found $3,200. The broadcast version said police found the money "in the woman's clothes," and White lamented that the most interesting part of the story had been left out.

Sometimes it helps, in this matter of taste, to have a dirty mind or to at least appreciate how you may sound to a person with a dirty mind. Thousands, perhaps millions, of such people may be listening. They may enjoy the joke, but your editor won't. Neither will management. Some angelic words suddenly become devilish when combined with certain other words. There is no place in a news script for double entendre. That's the province of Jay Leno.

On the other hand, don't be a Milquetoast. On the day the Dionne quintuplets were born, the writer of the Lowell Thomas program left the story out of his script—purposely. "It just didn't seem decent," he explained, "having five babies all at once." Thomas, consequently, was twenty-four hours late in reporting the greatest human interest story of the decade. Perhaps the best quote to come out of World War II was General McAuliffe's one-word reply, "Nuts!" when the Germans demanded his surrender at besieged Bastogne. A CBS News writer balked at using the direct quote! When the Lindberghs' first child was kidnapped on March 1, 1932, NBC News did not carry the story at first because it seemed "too sensational." And when President Truman called a music critic an "S.O.B.," all the networks had a fit deciding whether to use the direct quote. Our recollection is that they didn't.

A pretty good rule when deciding whether to quote anyone's profanity is to ask yourself: How important is it? If the statement is important enough to attract attention and perhaps find its way into the history books, then go with it. "Damn the torpedoes, full speed ahead."

The time has long since passed when adjectives denoting race or nationality could be used to describe persons accused of violating the law. The only exception is when the story loses much, if not all, of its significance when the race or nationality of the person is left out. For example, if police describe fully a man wanted for a bank robbery, and the journalist reports the wanted man's height, weight, and color of eyes, but does not report that he is Mexican and speaks with a strong Spanish accent, the description is practically worthless. Mention of race is appropriate and necessary when an African-American, an Hispanic, a female—or any combination thereof—is named to the president's cabinet or to any other high government post. In our society, this is news. The test is pertinence. Is the identification an integral part of the story? Is it news? If you can't decide, leave it out.

Never use terms for race or nationality that have connotations of contempt. Most of these abusive terms require no listing. They are well known. (It should be noted, however, that *Chinaman*, still heard occasionally, is derogatory. Say *Chinese*.)

Slang can pose problems. It is good to write naturally, as you speak, but you want at the same time to maintain some dignity. Every day we hear *buck* used as a synonym for *dollar*, but we would not write for broadcast "The mayor's salary was raised by five thousand bucks." Some slang phrases are really clichés—for example, "His advisers gave him a bum steer."

Slang is best suited for feature stories, especially sports. It should *never* appear in a story dealing with tragedy, where it adds a flippant tone.

A Note of Caution

Some flagrant violations of taste occur because the writer or producer of a sponsored show has not taken the trouble to learn who the sponsor is and where the commercials come in the program. It is appallingly bad taste to go, as one radio station did, from the report of a fire that claimed five lives to a commercial that began "For that hot, burning sensation. . . ." Know who is sponsoring your newscast. Know what the commercial says. If the story and commercial are incompatible, usually the commercial or the story, can be switched around. If a story "belongs" where it is because of its news value or context, then the commercial should give way. Occasionally the position of a story—the order in which it is read—is immaterial. In that case, the story can be shifted.

Sometimes the advertising agency, notified of a conflicting story, will want to cancel out of the program altogether. For example, if an airplane has crashed with heavy loss of life and an airline is sponsoring the broadcast, the airline probably will want to reschedule its commercials for another day. That's its privilege.

The juxtaposition of *any* tragedy with a "jolly" commercial is to be avoided. If necessary, insert another story between the report of the tragedy and the commercial. The listener and the sponsor will both appreciate it.

Care also should be exercised in interrupting the program in progress for a news bulletin. How important is the program? What kind of program is it? The career of an editor at one network was blighted because he interrupted an address by the president of the United States. Paul White confessed that he once broke into a program of dance music with a bulletin on the death of a great industrialist and how, to his horror, immediately after the bulletin he heard the full orchestra playing "I'll Be Glad When You're Dead, You Rascal You."

The opportunity for such embarrassment is much less at a local station, where there is likely to be closer coordination between the news and programming departments. Not so many people are involved.

"The Other Network"

Today, what you can say on the air includes mention of "the other network." For years, networks could not bring themselves to identify a competitor's program on the air. Now, in the attribution of a story, it is routine for the networks to name each other.

This "cross-fertilization" of news between networks most frequently occurs as a result of the Sunday panel shows. The guests on these programs usually are newsmakers, and the news they make is reported by all networks. With due credit the videotape is often shared.

So do not hesitate to quote, with proper attribution, from a story that is exclusive with another station or network. Some old-fashioned managers may object. If they do, try to convince them that news is news and ought to be reported.

Beware the Cliché

Once upon a time, in a network newsroom, the writers drew a map of a cliché-ridden continent washed on the east by the Restless Ocean, in which, clearly marked beside Desperate Straits, lay the Depths of Despair. The eastern shore was labeled Rockbound Coast. The largest country was Major Power, whose political capital, Mounting Tension, lay west of the Undulating Plains. You found the crime capital, Dull Thud, at the headwaters of a river called Meandering Stream, just before you come to Sorry Pass. Meandering Stream flowed south a thousand miles and emptied into the Widening Gulf. The principal metropolis on the West Coast was Crystal Clear, washed by the Great Expanse of Water. In the midst of this western ocean large X-marks indicated a score of Watery Graves. At the bottom of the map stretched the Sea of Upturned Faces.

Newscasters have always had fun with clichés. The late renowned CBS correspondent Winston Burdett told of how, in Tel Aviv, he joined correspondents from ABC and NBC in a contest to see who could make up the longest list of clichés found in dispatches from the Middle East. These included "the strategic 103-mile waterway" for the Suez Canal and "the uneasy head of the desert kingdom" for King Hussein of Jordan.

Too often it has been the "oil-rich" Middle East. It is also the Middle East "powder keg." One correspondent claims to have had a bad dream in which "roving bands of militant camels began kicking over powder kegs in the oil-rich Middle East." It was a real mess.

Use of such clichés may have been abetted by the old United Press rule that no person's name should be used in the lead sentence, so that the crucifixion of Christ would have been bulletined:

> JERUSALEM (SATURDAY)—UP—THE STRONG-WILLED BEARDED LEADER OF THE JEWISH REVOLUTIONARY SECT WAS EXECUTED YESTERDAY IN THE COMPANY OF TWO THIEVES.

Then, of course, there is the story of the witty UPI editor who cabled his correspondents: PLEASE, PLEASE AVOID CLICHÉS LIKE THE PLAGUE!

Russell Baker of the *New York Times* once did a wonderful column on indifference that was not callous, aggression that was not naked—"I had nearly decided that aggression never occurred with its clothes on"—and gall that was mitigated. As for *innocent victim,* he found a victim who, far from innocent, had just murdered his cousin.

An old journalistic cliché, smacking of British mystery stories, is *rumpled tweeds.* A writer for the *Saturday Review,* Dereck Williamson, said, "Not long ago I read in the *New York Times* that a man who liked to wear rumpled tweeds had died. The *Times,*" Williamson said, "gave no details—not a word about the kind of tweeds or who rumpled them. As the man was quite old, I assume he was a traditionalist who rumpled his own tweeds."

In a lead editorial in the *Times,* chickens came to roost in the White House and the president, after painting himself in a corner, sent his budget back to the drawing board. We are not trying to embarrass the *Times.* We wish only to demonstrate that clichés are sneaky—they creep in. (You may even find one or two in this text.)

Editors abhor clichés. When he was anchoring the news, Walter Cronkite once asked a writer to wrap up several stormy weather developments, saying, "You know, a Mother Nature-on-the-rampage sort of thing." The writer knew enough not to give Cronkite what he literally asked for. He would have got hung (repeat *hung*) if he had, Mother Nature being the *grande dame* among clichés. Instead, he wrote, "Nature caused trouble today across much of the country." And Cronkite bought it.

Phrases that once were fresh become clichés through overuse. Thus, in the early 1960s, we had "break-away Katanga" to describe a province that seceded from the Congo. The second half of the decade brought civil war to Nigeria and another cliché, "break-away Biafra." Now, in the 1990s, we have the "break-away" states in the Balkans. Sensitive writers catch themselves humming these clichés as if they were jingles.

Widespread usage converts brightness into triteness. Barbara Ward demonstrated insight in 1966 when she drew an analogy between the problems of our planet and those of people in a spaceship. By the end of the decade the title of her book, *Spaceship Earth,* had been so overworked it was hackneyed.

A writer once looked up from his desk and asked, "Is there such a thing as election fever?"

'I don't think so,'' a colleague deadpanned. "But call the hospitals and find out.''
It's a fever which has infected many scripts.

Avoid the phrase *remains to be seen*, so often heard in interpretive reporting. Instead, try saying something like "No one knows the outcome'' or "It's hard to tell what happens next.'' Save *remains to be seen* for that body under glass in Red Square.

Test your phrases for aptness and freshness. Both are required in good writing. You should be able to hear how sentences will sound when spoken. Morley Safer of "60 Minutes'' speaks of "the marvelous music of the English language.''

The writer who commits a cliché must expect a degree of ridicule, if not censure. One radio writer, who shall be nameless, managed this awesome mixture of metaphors and clichés in a single sentence:

> The revolt in France during May and June has come home to roost, and it's right in the lap of the French taxpayer.

That writer was ridiculed *and* censured.

Watch out for anatomical clichés:

finger in the pie
foot in his mouth
foot in the door
ear to the ground
nose to the grindstone

And synonyms for the proper names of cities are apt to be clichés:

the City of Light (Paris)
the Eternal City (Rome)
the Film Capital (Hollywood)
Bean Town (Boston)
the City of Brotherly Love (Philadelphia)
the nation's capital (Washington)
the Windy City (Chicago)

Herewith a gallery of other clichés. It does not pretend to be complete, but they're some of the bromides heard most often in news broadcasts:

augurs well	blast (as in *bombing*)
bids fair	crystal clear
curb (for *restrict, restrain, reduce*)	mute evidence
doing as well as can be expected	no uncertain terms

easy prey	pack (as in hurricane-*pack-ing* winds)
few and far between	predawn attack
gone but not forgotten	probe (for *investigate*)
hail of bullets	pulverize (as in *bombing*)
hale and hearty	roving bands
here at home	selling like hotcakes
hold a parley	slate a speech
in my judgment	thick and fast
it all began	top advisers
last but not least	uneasy truce
leaps and bounds	violence flared
loud and clear	vital stake
massive attack	white stuff (for *snow*)
mounting tension	widespread fear
	worse for wear

And *never* let anyone "leave in a huff." That was a hackneyed expression more than fifty years ago when Paul White observed that the Huff must be, without question, America's most popular car.

Other Words to Watch Out For

Be careful of the word *casualty*. In his book *To Kill a Messenger,* Bill Small mentions Pentagon distress over the fact that the public, hearing a broadcaster report casualties during the Vietnam War, did not seem to realize *casualties* included dead *and* wounded. Indeed, *casualties* may refer *only* to wounded. Many listeners think the word refers only to people who are killed. Take care in your copy to avoid this misunderstanding. And remember the difference between *wounded* and *injured:* you are *injured* in a fall from a ladder; you are *wounded* by a machinegun bullet. Example: On May 18, 1992, when troops in Bangkok opened fire on pro-democracy demonstrators, a CBS correspondent reported "hundreds injured and many killed." Certainly the demonstrators suffered injuries, but, more specifically, they were *wounded.* Webster's first definition of *wound* is "to hurt by violence," and the example given is "as to wound an enemy with a sword."

Especially in journalism, precision is to be treasured. Choose the word with the most specific meaning.

Be sure you know the meaning—the implications—of the words you use. For example, be careful of the verb *point out.* When you say so-and-so "pointed out" that such-and-such was the case, you present the statement as gospel. The same goes for *disclose.* Only something that exists can be disclosed.

Be aware of the nuances of words. During World War II, for example, it was always "Washington says" and "Berlin claims." Western reporters today have Baghdad and Beijing "claiming" much more frequently than London or Washington. It's the other side that claims.

The late Theodore Bernstein of the *New York Times* was a purist when it came to the use of *claim*. In his book *The Careful Writer* he agreed with H. L. Mencken that *claim*, in the sense of *assert*, is newspaper jargon. He said, "The verb *claim* should not be used as a synonym for *say, assert*, or *declare* except when there is at issue an assertion of a right, title, or the like." Webster's agrees. Watch for the shades of meaning words can convey.

Remember that *state* is not a synonym for *say*. According to Webster's, *to state* is "to set forth in detail." The first two definitions given for *to state* in the *Random House Dictionary of the English Language* are "to declare definitely or specifically" and "to set forth formally in speech or writing." *State* is one of the most frequently misused words heard on the air.

Two other pairs of frequently misused words are *robbery* and *theft* and *prison* and *jail*. A robbery is attended by violence or threat of violence. The victim is held up, for example, at the point of a gun; theft, the act of stealing, is accompanied by stealth. A jail is for minor offenders; a prison usually is a place of confinement for persons convicted of more serious crimes. Murderers are sentenced to a term in prison, not jail.

A word overworked as a bridge between stories is *meanwhile*. This adverb should be used only when a close relationship exists in subject matter, and an overlap in time actually is meant. You'll be amazed how well you can get along without this crutch.

Avoid Latin prefix words like *semi-starved, pre-armistice, transmit*, and *conclude*. Instead, use *half-starved, before the armistice, send* (so much better than *transmit* or *dispatch*) and *finish* or *end*.

Verbs to Avoid

Jack Hart, the writing coach for *The Oregonian*, berates writers who, by using weak verbs, "squeeze the life out of an action-filled world." So, try to avoid forms of the verb *to be—is, was, are, were—*for they are the weakest of all verbs. Of course, you will use them. It's inevitable. (We just did.) But notice how much other, stronger verbs can contribute:

She was the winner.
She won.

He was proud of it.
He took pride in it.

There was another fire there tonight.
Fire broke out there again tonight. . . .

And think twice about using the colorless, terribly overworked verb *continue*. You can usually replace it with a verb that says more. "The talks dragged on past midnight" is better than "The talks continued past midnight."

Those Latin Words

In writing the plural of nouns taken directly from the Latin, employ the letter "s" in the following:

> *curriculums,* not *curricula*
> *dictums,* not *dicta*
> *honorariums,* not *honoraria*
> *referendums,* not *referenda*
> *stadiums,* not *stadia*
> *ultimatums,* not *ultimata*

Ad hoc, sine qua non, per diem, and *quid pro quo* are out. Not all your listeners know Latin. But *data* and *memoranda* are still in.

Medium, as in *television medium,* is a Latin word. It is singular, although you'd be surprised how many people confuse it with *media,* which is plural. As Theodore Bernstein said, "Unless you suffer from the present-day AD-DICTION, the singular is still *medium* and the plural *media.*"

Don't be afraid to use the same word twice, or three or four times, if it is the *right* word. Your broadcast style should be natural, not contrived. At one station the anchor, anxious for variety, reported the arrest of three suspects. During the telling of the story, the suspects first were "arrested," then "apprehended," then seized. Finally, they were "scooped up!"

During World War II, Paul White posted this memo in the CBS newsroom:

> This morning within the space of 30 seconds I heard German submarines called *submarines, U-boats, submersibles* and *underseas craft.* The word *submarines* was used once. It should have been used more often. But, my God, *submersibles!* That word should never be used at all.

Jesse Zousmer, who, after leaving CBS, became vice-president in charge of television news at ABC, believed that when someone said something, the writer should use *said*—not *stated, added, asserted,* or *averred.* Anyway, better synonyms for *said* are *announced, promised, warned,* or *insisted.* But be sure these synonyms apply.

That is, there must have been an announcement, a promise, a warning, or an insistence on what was said.

No Moon-Tailed Peacocks

In "telling" the news, go easy on adjectives. The adjectives you do use should be selected not only for accuracy but for their quality. Is the adjective unfamiliar to listeners? Is it pedantic? Logan Pearsall Smith lamented, "Why wasn't I born, alas, in an age of Adjectives; why can one no longer write of silver-shedding Tears and moon-tailed Peacocks? Of eloquent Death?"

The answer for broadcast journalists is easy. No one talks that way, and there's no time for all the fancy stuff. Don't try to be erudite in the use of adjectives. Never write, as a novelist once did, that the eggs were fried longer "to coagulate their mucosity." Such writing is pretentious—it can't possibly be conversational. (We admit we chose an extreme example, but you get the idea.)

The bigger the story, the fewer adjectives you need—the force is in the facts. No broadcaster ever used fewer adjectives than Ed Murrow. The strength of his language lay in the choice of nouns and verbs.

ABC News once directed its writers to use no more than one adjective per noun. This may have been too arbitrary, but it is worth thinking about. Such a guideline would have prevented a writer for WCBS, New York, from confusing his listeners in reporting the aftereffects of a break in a water main. He said, "It may be weeks before the 48-inch water main break is repaired." He didn't tell his listeners whether he was talking about a *48-inch main* or a *48-inch break.*

A word of caution about *very,* which can be used either as an adjective or adverb. As an adverb it is overworked. Every time you are tempted to write *very,* try the sentence without it. You'll be (very) pleasantly surprised.

And take care in the use of superlatives. Think before describing something as the smallest or the biggest, or the first or the last. Too often reporters using superlatives are trusting their memory: they can't remember seeing, or hearing of, a bigger fire or a worse flood. But memories are faulty. Editors have told us that about half the superlatives in a script, when checked, turn out to be either questionable or demonstrably not true.

Every superlative should carry a winking red light.

A word about the use in broadcasting of the adjective *live:* don't use it as in "Our Washington correspondent is standing by live." Such use of the adjective is nonsense. As Mervin Block, the writing coach, observed upon hearing a similar line, "Always good to hear that reporters standing by are alive."

Mark Twain gave the best advice on the use of adjectives: "As to the adjective, when in doubt, strike it out."

Prepositions Can Help

Prepositions can help in a special way. They can be used to break up unnatural "freight train" phrases. Here, for example, is how a little preposition can help. Instead of saying "He cited the public's long-term natural resources interest," insert the preposition *in* and make it read "He cited the public's long-term interest in natural resources."

Used in this way, prepositions break phrases into manageable pieces that the ear—the mind, really—more readily accepts. They increase readability AND understanding.

That Is More Conversational

As your broadcast style develops, you will find yourself making more use of the relative pronoun *that*. This is a good sign. In speech, *that* is used more often than *which*. It's more conversational. And broadcast style is the style of conversation.

On the other hand, *which* is sometimes preferable, though the rules are confusing. Fowler himself calls the distinctions made between *that* and *which* "an odd jumble." According to American grammarians, *which* is correct when the relative clause is non-defining; *that* is correct when the clause defines. This sentence illustrates the correct use of each: "One of the nations *that* emerged was Vietnam, *which* later was partitioned."

The point is that clauses properly begun with *which* appear more often in print than they do in speech. Long sentences tend to have such clauses. So if you are using *which* less often, you should, as a writer for the broadcast media, be enjoying it more.

Thirty years after it was first published, Eric Sevareid's memoir, *Not So Wild a Dream,* appeared in a new edition. In his new introduction Sevareid talked of his writing style in the first edition. He said, "I alone, apparently, am bothered—to this day—by the use throughout the book of *which* where *that* would fall more gently on the ear."

Pay close attention, always, to sound. To the smoothness—the gentleness—with which the sentence flows.

So much for *that* as a relative pronoun. *That* is also used as a conjunction. For example, "It means *that* no law can be passed" and "He said *that* he would vote." In the interest of tight writing, this conjunction often—not always—can be eliminated. "It means no law can be passed" and "He said he would vote" read perfectly well, and make perfectly good sense, without the *that*.

But sometimes the *that* is helpful. For example: "He emphasized *that* the figures have been published" is better than "He emphasized the figures have been published." This is because the listener, hearing *he emphasized the figures*, gets a meaning quite different from the meaning of the entire sentence. The listener is led off in one direction, only to be abruptly turned around by the last words, *have been published*. The listener is misled for a very short time—perhaps only a second—but there was no reason to mislead at all.

A Word for the Wise

A most serviceable word is *almost*. The late A. J. Leibling, that astute critic of American journalism, once said, "*Almost* is a very unsatisfactory word, but writers almost never use it sufficiently. It sounds better to say things without qualification, but that is very seldom justified."

A very important word, *almost*.

Those Weather People

Next to sportscasters, the worst handlers of words are the weather reporters. Edwin Newman tells of the meteorologist who predicted, "Tomorrow night, temperatures will gradually plummet." Another, venturing hazardously into the area of hard news, reported that a river was low: "it had low water levelwise." Weather people talk about "shower activity" instead of showers and "snow activity" instead of snow. And exactly what is "cloud activity?" The word *activity*, they think, makes them sound more important.

One of the country's best-known forecasters on television, an authentic meteorologist, spoke of "winds out of a northwesterly direction." Why not "winds out of the northwest"? Weather reporters like to say "precip" instead of precipitation and "temp" instead of temperature—"High temps today in the upper 70's." One weatherman predicted that the afternoon high would be near 80 degrees. Unfortunately, he made that prediction at 6 P.M., after the afternoon had come and gone. He was not thinking.

Danger Words

Use these words with caution. Any one of them could lead to accusations of libel.

admit, confess
atheist
blackmail
bribe, bribery
communist, fascist
defraud, fraud
illegitimate

incompetent
racist
suicide
swindle

Gender Neutral Language

The women's liberation movement has affected language. No longer is it acceptable to refer to news*man*, camera*man*, and anchor*man* in the generic sense. Today, thankfully, there are enough women in broadcast journalism for those words to be inappropriate. For *newsman, reporter, correspondent, producer,* or *editor* may be substituted. *Photographer* may be substituted for *cameraman. Anchor* or *anchorwoman* may be substituted for *anchorman.*

Some editors prefer *chairperson* to *chairman, chairwoman,* or *chair,* and *congressperson* to *congressman* or *congresswoman.* While the use of *congressman* in referring to a woman is indefensible, it is proper to refer to a woman who is a member of Congress as a ''congresswoman.'' Also, if the operator of a camera is a man, it is proper to call him a ''cameraman.'' (You don't *have* to call him a cameraman; as in the case of a woman, he may be called a ''photographer.'' There is flexibility.) *Businesswoman* remains the principal substitute for *businessman.*

Airlines have abandoned the word *stewardess.* They use, instead, *flight attendants.* Some people prefer that waitresses be referred to as ''servers.'' A good many women, and some men, regard the words *man* (for human being, as in ''Man does not live by bread alone'') and *mankind* as chauvinist. Why not, they argue, speak instead of humanity and the human race? There's no reason not to, if the language comes gracefully. But for many writers, *man* and *mankind* are still good words.

A major change in many newsrooms was the decision to drop the traditional use of *Miss* or *Mrs.* with a woman's last name. The argument was that since a man's marital status is not revealed in *Mr.,* why treat women differently? The argument makes sense. There are times, however, when confusion arises because a husband and wife, sister and brother, father and daughter, have the same surname. Usually you can write around this. You can use *father, mother, wife, husband, son, daughter,* or whatever, without using the surname. William Safire says *Ms.* is fine, except when the woman signifies a preference for the marital status to be known. Then, he says, use *Mrs.* or *Miss.*

Spokesperson and *spokeswoman* are frequently used as alternatives to *spokesman.* Generally, persons who fight fires should be called *firefighters,* though we see no harm in calling a male member of the fire department a *fireman.* Generically speaking, *mail carrier* is preferable to *mailman,* but if the person delivering the mail is a man, *mailman* would seem acceptable.

The National Organization for Women (NOW) advocates the use of the gender-neutral words *ancestors* for *forefathers* and *city leaders* for *city fathers.* Some revisions, like *womyn* for *women* and *waitron* for *waitress,* are far out.

Language always is in a state of evolution, and this business of titles for women in the news is in an awkward stage. A few years from now, philologists will be able to say, on the basis of established usage, what is right in this respect. Until then, do as your news director tells you.

The Sound of Words

The public never sees your words. You are writing for the ear, so think always of the *sound* of what you write. This applies not only to the sound of each word but to the sound of combinations of words.

During the wedding of Princess Margaret the late British broadcaster, Richard Dimbleby, described Queen Elizabeth's tenseness and "the comforting, tall, friendly and alert figure of the Duke of Edinburgh, on whose right arm she could rely." These words are fastened together, not only by meaning, but by a thread of sound, notably the *l*'s in *tall, friendly, alert,* and *rely.* No less effective are the *f*'s in *comforting, friendly,* and *figure* and the *r*'s that recur from *comforting* all the way through to *rely.* The sounds are subtly woven together to make a whole fabric, so that the listener, liking the sentence, is not aware how alliteration has been used. If you contrive such sentences, they fail. They must come to you out of a sensitivity of how words sound. They spring from your subconscious in harmonious array.

Good sentences are written by writers who *listen* to the words. Watch them as they write and you will see them reading what they have just written, most of them reading aloud, usually in a whisper, testing each phrase, each sentence, each sequence of sentences for sound.

Incidentally, an odd-sounding, much overused formula to be avoided is that which, by modifying a person's last name by his or her age (*x*-year-old) makes the person seem to be a thing. Thus, we had reference to "the 78-year-old Ball" when comic Lucille Ball died, and reference to Claude Fly, an American agronomist kidnapped by Tupamaros guerrillas in Uruguay, as "the 66-year-old Fly." These expressions are unnatural enough in print (who ever talks that way?) but, aurally, they are absurd.

Do not hesitate to rewrite—if you have time. Professionals are constantly rewriting copy, especially their leads. A visiting journalism student once expressed surprise that Murrow's writer was preparing parts of the 7:45 P.M. script at one o'clock in the afternoon. The writer was "putting stories in the bank" so that he would have time to deal adequately with stories that might break in the hour or two before Murrow went on the air. By starting early, he *made* time in which to rewrite. And one of the reasons you rewrite is to make the copy sound right—to make it flow.

Just as some people are tone deaf regarding music, some writers are deaf to the "tones"—and "overtones"—of words. The result is ineffective writing. Listen carefully to the reports of major broadcasters if you are sensitive to how words sound. Notice how often their sentences end with strong nouns or verbs and how rarely they end with pronouns, adjectives, or adverbs, which tend to make sentences seem to peter out. A strong, meaningful last word gives a sentence definition. You seem to hear the period. And listen to the rhythm in their sentences. One short declarative sentence after another is monotonous. After a couple of these sentences, try to start the next sentence with an *and* or a *but*. Then, after that sentence, go back to the simple declarative. Maintain rhythm.

Shy away from sibilants, especially in succession. (Read that last sentence aloud, real fast, and you will see why!) Don't give the broadcaster—or yourself—a line like, "She asserted she was seeking new assistance." Avoid words that slip and slide.

Many sibilants can be avoided simply by dropping unnecessary *s*'s at the end of words. It is better, for example, to write:

> "The effect of the *House* action" rather than "the effect of the *House's* action."
> "The cosmonauts will make a *two-week* visit to the United States" instead of "The cosmonauts will make a *two-week's* visit to the United States."
> "No *sign* of cooperation" instead of "no *signs* of cooperation."
> "He expressed his *hope* for the future" instead of "He expressed his *hopes* for the future."
> "She said nothing in *regard* to policy" instead of "She said nothing in *regards* to policy."
> "He had no *intention* of going" instead of "He had no *intentions* of going."

And, incidentally, don't say "*Damages* were estimated at two million dollars." Say "*Damage* was estimated at two million dollars." You sue for *damages*.

Sound-Alikes

Be careful in the use of words that sound alike. How misleading such sound-alikes can be was demonstrated when a secretary, transcribing a correspondent's report, quoted him as saying, "That's partly why they excepted Congressman Michael Harrington's amendment." The correspondent had said, "That's partly why they *accepted* Congressman Michael Harrington's amendment."

And think how this sounds: "The Cleveland Indians scored two runs, the Boston Red Sox *one.*" The writer of a line like that might be saved if the score were flashed on the TV screen. But what if the listener was listening to his car radio?

Through and *threw* are two other words that can confuse. "He *threw* out the ball *throughout* the ball game."

Flout and *flaunt*.

And *sex* and *sect*.

Roger Mudd told the story of how a politician had fun with words that sound alike—at the expense of his opponent. It happened in 1950 when Senator Claude Pepper was opposed by his protége, George Smathers. According to Mudd, "The most famous speech of that campaign was Smathers' play to the wool-hats of North Florida. 'Are you aware,' Smathers asked his rural audience, 'that Claude Pepper is known all over Washington as a shameless extrovert? Not only that, but this man is reliably reported to practice nepotism with his sister-in-law and that his own sister was once a thespian in New York? Worst of all, it's established that Mr. Pepper, before his marriage, practiced celibacy.' " Mudd concluded by saying, "Someone said that Claude Pepper became, on that day, history's first victim of 'guilt by assonance.' " (We had to look up *assonance*. It means "resemblance of sound.")

Sometimes reporters have fun with words. A serious newsman who occasionally breaks into verse on the air is Charles Osgood. After two prominent congressmen had to resign because of sex scandals, he observed on his morning program:

One robin does not a springtime make,
One swallow no summer at all,
But a point one can make
Without fear of mistake—
One lark has brought many a fall.

It is *unintentional* humor you must guard against. I think of the reporter who said a woman was shot "by her bay window," instead of "as she stood by" her bay window. Doug Ramsey of the Foundation for American Communications cites this one: "A 29-year-old woman attempted suicide today when she leaped from the Yakima River bridge. A passing motorist said he saw her jump through his rearview mirror." The BBC warns its writers in this regard and gives as an example the broadcaster who, reporting a benefit golf tournament, said, "Lady Dorothy played a round with the prime minister."

Think of what you are saying, or *appear* to be saying. Think of the meaning of what you say. The literal meaning.

Two Things

"About the best I can do to be the least bit helpful is to say a little bit about two things." The speaker was Charles Osgood, addressing a meeting of radio and television news directors. "Thing One," he said, "is the English language. Thing Two is blurred images."

He was blunt. There was no word shortage, he said. ''I've caught enough of your broadcasts. . . . Every news broadcast and every story is stuffed with words. Over-stuffed sometimes. But don't you suspect that some of those words—maybe even most of them—aren't getting through?

''It's a depressing thought,'' he said, ''but there is evidence that many of the words follow a trajectory that takes them into the ear of the listener and out the other one without passing through the brain. Bloated words and phrases don't penetrate. Well-chosen, well-ordered ones do.''

Amen.

6. *Some Grammatical Goblins*

Curb verbal abuse. Here are some of the grammatical goblins that may haunt you:

We start with the verbs *lie* and *lay*. There was a boy who shouted to his dog, "Lay down!" The dog, being extremely intelligent and well trained, didn't move. It knew a dog *lies* down.

When you go to bed, you *lie* down. *Lay* implies a direct object. The dog *lays* his head in your lap. You *lay* your book on the table. After you do that, the book *lies* there. In your writing, distinguish between *lie* and *lay*.

Some reporters—too many—blunder into using adjectives for adverbs. Here are some samples taken off the air:

> "It turned out beautiful (beautifully)."
> "Subsidies permit Airbus to sell its planes more cheap (cheaply)."
> "[The shuttle] landed perfect (perfectly)."
> "Almost all of them performed bad (badly)."
> "The vote turned out favorable (favorably)."
> "She can do that good (well)."

This misuse of *good* is growing, especially in sports reporting where sentences like "He hits good" and "He shoots good" are common. Commercials don't help. Ectotrin, for example, boasts that it "works safer," not more safely.

Advertisers and too many newswriters are scorning the accusative *whom*. "When you need a laxative," asks Exlax, "who do you trust?" Similarly in news scripts we find "children who they'll be adopting" and "candidates who the voters favor." In all three instances, of course, *who* is wrong. The test for *who* and *whom* is simple.

If the relative pronoun is the object of a transitive verb like *adopt* or *favor,* it's *whom.*

In May 1991, President Bush was diagnosed as suffering from Graves' disease, a condition that produces an irregular heartbeat. He responded to treatment, and a local TV reporter said, "It seems like the President is doing just fine." Here the word *like* is used incorrectly as a conjunction. This is what dictionaries call nonstandard usage. The reporter should have said, "It seems as though the President is doing just fine." Or, still better, "It seems the President is doing just fine."

Whenever you are tempted to say something like "It looks like the bill will pass" or "It happened just like they predicted," remember you are using language that is off the mark. Use *as though* or simply *as.* "It looks as though the bill will pass" and "It happened just as they predicted."

If you want to be a first-class writer, don't confuse *farther* and *further.* The first relates to distance; the second to degree or extent. For example:

They moved farther north.
The police will investigate further.

If you can't decide which to use, remember that the one for distance starts with *far.*

We have to level with you. Increasingly, at the cost of precision in communicating, *farther* and *further* are being used interchangeably. The same is happening with *jail* and *prison,* and *robbery* and *theft,* whose basic differences we explained earlier. This trend toward dilution of meaning is dangerous, and we hope, as a respecter of language, you will resist.

A word about *hopefully.* Originally, the adverb meant "in a hopeful manner," as in "He entered hopefully upon his quest." Today, in most instances, the word expresses hope on the part of the person writing or speaking: "Hopefully, the Red Sox will win." We like what William Morrow's *Reference Book of Grammar & Usage* says on this subject: "Since careful speakers and writers frown on this [second] usage, it would be wise to avoid it when you think it might annoy your audience." Or, we would add, cause your audience to think you don't know better. You decide.

Good usage demands that two or more words combined to form an adjective be hyphenated. Example: "She works a forty-hour week." However, TV producers by the hundreds violate this rule when, in the weather portion of their programs, they omit the hyphen in "seven-day forecast." (Or the forecast for five or six days, as the case may be.)

The most grievous grammatical mistake cropping up in newscasts today is the one you would least expect because the rule is so simple: Prepositions and transitive verbs—that is, verbs that take a direct object—require the accusative case. A bare-bones example: He hit me. The transitive verb is *hit,* and the object in the accusative case is *me.*

So simple, yet some reporters are confused, else we would not have heard them say:

> "They approached the photographer and I."
> "The bus waited for him and I."
> "There had been an argument between she and her son."
> "There were no special differences between he and Gorbachev."
> "It involved he and Tony Perez."
> "Efforts were being made to find out for who and by who the medals were left."

For sure, the writer of that last example gets no medal.

It seems incredible that for a significant number of newscasters such a rule of grammar has proved difficult. Difficult, too, for others. Well-educated people commit the same atrocity. A member of the Senate Judiciary Committee, during a break in the Clarence Thomas hearings, told reporters in mellifluous voice, "Most members are like I."

One hopes not.

7. *Keeping It Short*

A long time ago, Mark Twain, giving advice to writers, said: "Use the right word, not its second cousin. Eschew surplusage—but do not omit necessary detail. Avoid slovenliness of form. Use good grammar. Employ a simple and straightforward style."

This is good instruction for journalism in all its forms. But the dictums that apply especially to broadcast journalism are 1) eschew surplusage—don't waste words— and 2) employ a simple and straightforward style. In an interview on "Today," William Saroyan said, "Good writing is irresistibly simple." Each sentence you write for broadcast should be sweet simplicity—deceptively simple and easy to understand. Because you are writing for the ear, the most transitory of all senses, you must use language in a special way. It makes no difference how good a reporter you are if the story you are reporting is not understood. And surplusage—wordiness—is particularly offensive in broadcast journalism where, literally, every second counts.

"Write Tight!"

"Write tight!" is the most common injunction heard in a broadcast newsroom. You must tell your stories in the fewest possible words. It means, as one news director has said, "boiling down a flood of information into a concise meaningful trickle." To do this expertly requires judgment. You must choose—select out—from your notes, or from the wire story, or both, what is essential. You must recognize what is basic, what gives the story meaning. And you must know what words to use in order to be succinct. For example, the sentence, "He wanted to know the reason for her departure," should sound wrong to you. Besides being pretentious, it takes almost twice as much time to read as "He wanted to know why she left." Your choice of words is all-important.

The best language is simple. Here is some simple language Charles Osgood used in a radio piece about a monastery. Referring to the monks, he said, "They live here. And when they die, they're buried here." His last line—always an important line—was "Peace is a tall order, but quiet is a place to start." Then there was his interview with an astronomer, a conversation in which they discussed the wonders to be found in interstellar space. What do you say for a "button" to such an interview? Here's what Osgood said:

> In our galaxy alone there are a hundred billion stars stretched out across a space so vast it would take a beam of light a hundred thousand years to cross. The wonder is that all those stars, and all that space, can fit into so small a place as the mind of man.

Fifty-three words. Only one word, *galaxy*, more than two syllables.
In World War II, in North Africa, Murrow captured a scene in fifteen seconds.

> Where the road cuts down to meet the stream there is a knocked-out tank, two dead men beside it and two more digging a grave. A little farther along, a German soldier sits smiling against the bank. He is covered with dust, and he is dead.

During the Korean War, Murrow had to write a few words to go with some film that showed American forces digging foxholes in the side of a hill. The voice-over he wrote was "If you dig before dark, you have a better chance of living after light."

The famous editor Herbert Bayard Swope once pointed out that history's best example of compressing a story appears in the Gospel of St. John, in the shortest verse in the Bible which reads, "Jesus wept." Swope said that in those two words John told a great deal more than if he had used hundreds of words, "because he allied himself with the imagination of the reader."

Ed Murrow was raised on the Bible and influenced by its language. On a bombing mission over Berlin his plane was buffeted by exploding antiaircraft shells. Murrow was scared. He wrote, "And I was very frightened," a paraphrase of the Bible's "And they were sore afraid." In five words, and in his reading of them, he conveyed—vividly—his fright. He allied himself with the imagination of the listener. And you recall the applause he heard at Buchenwald—"It sounded like the hand-clapping of babies, they were so weak."

Morley Safer captured the essence of the Vietnam War in a sentence. He described the amassing of American munitions and equipment against the enemy and added, "Somewhere on foot, rifle in hand, is the enemy." The incisive sentence is not fancy. Most often it is plain, like the edge of a knife. When the Gulf War started,

CNN's Bernard Shaw and two of his colleagues looked out their hotel room in Baghdad and saw the sky filled with antiaircraft fire. All around them the sirens screamed, and they could hear, in the distance, bombs exploding. Shaw said, when he got on the air, "I've never been there, but it feels like we are in the center of hell."

There is power in simplicity, in language that is well chosen and lean.

But these stories, you say, are not typical. War, because of its very nature, lends itself to strong language, to writing that "grabs." This is true, but creativity, and impact, are possible with stories that are much more mundane. With thought you *can* lift your writing out of the ordinary. Here are some examples:

When scientists were about to activate the revolutionary Hubble telescope, Osgood said, "This is the day the Hubble telescope opens its window on the stars."

Reporting on the tight job market, Tom Brokaw of NBC could have said something like "Today, if you are unemployed, it's hard to get a job." Instead, he said, "Finding a job in this recession is full-time work."

On the fiftieth anniversary of Winston Churchill's famous Iron Curtain speech in Fulton, Missouri, CBS's Bruce Morton referred to "the Iron Curtain laid down across Europe" as "the phrase that announced the Cold War." The whole thought was strengthened by the verb *announced*.

Match your enterprise in reporting with enterprise in the use of words, remembering that short everyday words are best.

Tight writing is not only for hard news and feature essays. If possible, documentary writing must be tighter still. For no problem in documentary production is more acute than the problem of finding time within the half-hour or hour for adequate examination of the issues. Test these opening lines from the CBS classic, "Harvest of Shame." Do you see a sentence, a phrase, a single word that does not serve a useful purpose?

> MURROW: This is an American story that begins in Florida and ends in New Jersey and New York State with the harvest. It is a 1960 *Grapes of Wrath* that begins at the Mexican border in California and ends in Oregon and Washington. It is the story of men and women and children who work 136 days of the year and average 900 dollars a year. They travel in buses. They ride trucks. They follow the sun.

The question regarding the expendability of any of this language was rhetorical. The documentary, produced by Fred W. Friendly and David Lowe, was an exposé of the shameful treatment of migrant workers in America. In these six simple declarative sentences, Ed Murrow set the scene.

One of the best writers in television news was the late Alice Weel Bigart. In 1968, when Ford's Theater was reopened in Washington, she wrote the script for a one-hour CBS special narrated by Roger Mudd. At the top of the show, the producer, Don Hewitt, allowed her one minute to tell (with visuals) the whole story of Lincoln's assassination, including the escape and capture of John Wilkes Booth. Also, in the same minute, she was to provide an introduction to what was happening then, 103 years later.

When you read this, note the wealth of specific detail Bigart managed, almost incredibly, to cram into a minute. The detail is executed—written—with such craftsmanship that, instead of being a jumble of incidentals, it reads beautifully and heightens interest. The sentences pack information, but they are lucid.

MUDD (PAN DOWN HANDBILL, MUSIC BEHIND): LINCOLN'S ATTENDANCE AT FORD'S THEATER ATTRACTED A NEAR CAPACITY HOUSE. IT ALSO ATTRACTED JOHN WILKES BOOTH. IT HAPPENED NEAR THE CLOSE OF ACT 3, SCENE 2. HARRY HAWK, THE ACTOR, HAD JUST DELIVERED THIS RIB-TICKLER: "WELL, I GUESS I KNOW ENOUGH TO TURN YOU INSIDE OUT, OLD GAL—YOU OLD SOCKDOLOGIZING OLD MANTRAP."

DISSOLVE TO ASSASSINATION SKETCH IN BOX 8, AS LAUGHTER RANG OUT, SO DID A SHOT. THIS CONTEMPORARY SKETCH SHOWS THE PRESIDENT, UNGUARDED, SITTING NEXT TO HIS WIFE. BOOTH FIRED ONCE AT CLOSE RANGE. LINCOLN NEVER REGAINED CONSCIOUSNESS.

DISSOLVE THROUGH TWO SKETCHES OF BOOTH'S ESCAPE AS THE PRESIDENT SLUMPED FORWARD, THE AGILE BOOTH ESCAPED BY JUMPING ONTO THE STAGE, 10 FEET BELOW. BUT HE BROKE A SHINBONE IN HIS FALL, AND WAS FINALLY TRAPPED AND SHOT TO DEATH IN A TOBACCO SHED IN VIRGINIA.

DEATH SCENE SKETCH THE DYING PRESIDENT WAS CARRIED ACROSS THE STREET, WHERE HIS LONG BODY WAS PLACED ON A BED IN THE HOME OF WILLIAM PETERSON, A TAILOR. DEATH CAME AT 7:22 IN THE MORNING, NINE HOURS AFTER THAT FINAL ACT AT FORD'S THEATER ON APRIL 14TH, 1865. NOW, FIVE SCORE AND THREE YEARS LATER, THE WORLD NOTES AND REMEMBERS.

The script is a demonstration that brevity—tightness in writing—does not mean wholesale sacrificing of detail. The trick lies in the *selection* of detail. Notice how skillfully the writer, after telling the story of the assassination in about fifty seconds, brings the viewer back to the theater by saying that death came "nine hours after that final act at Ford's Theater on April 14th, 1865." She is now ready, in just twelve words, to set the viewer up for the next scene—the gala reopening—which is in the present: "Now, five score and three years later, the world notes and remembers," language that recalls Lincoln's Gettysburg Address.

This is tight, professional writing. Alice Weel Bigart knew the advantage gained by using a simple and straightforward style.

"Today, at Mount Sinai . . ."

Mark Twain also cautioned against the omission of necessary detail. One thinks of the story of how, if Moses should present the Ten Commandments today, a newscaster's lead might be: "Today, at Mount Sinai, Moses came down with ten commandments, the most important three of which are . . ."

In writing a news story, do not simplify—tighten—by leaving out basic elements. Sure you are pressed for time. The cliché is right—time *is* a tyrant. Nowhere more than in broadcasting. But abbreviation must never be at the expense of meaning. Sense is not to be sacrificed for the facile phrase. Distortion is not—repeat *not*—excusable "because it's simpler this way" or "because this way it reads better." You must cover what is essential and, with skill, *make* it read.

In "keeping it tight" you are selecting what to report. That is why, as a news writer, you are an editor, too, with all the responsibility that editorship entails. The amount of background information which can be included in any news story is limited. In broadcast news there is not the room—time—for background that exists in print journalism. When a story has been in the news for days, even weeks, it is assumed that the listener knows the background. Only the latest developments in these so-called "running" stories are reported.

The cut-off date for providing such background information is, inevitably, arbitrary. You decide one day, in reporting the story, that by this time the basic facts are generally known. You must, in your judgment, be quite sure of this. There's no use reporting the story if you leave out the background that enables the listener to know what the story really is all about.

Strive always for clarity. Simplicity of language and clarity, which come from clear thinking, go hand in hand. Bill Small, the broadcast veteran who teaches at Fordham, says, "Good television journalism presents news in the most attractive and lucid form yet devised by man." In TV, the attractiveness and lucidity depend on the use made of words and pictures. In radio, they depend on the use made of words alone. And neither sentences nor visual sequences can be long drawn out, discursive, or diffuse. In both media, tight editing applies.

These are generalities. Let's be specific with another example. It's a UPI story on the scattering of the ashes of Carl Sandburg.

> GALESBURG, ILL. (UPI) CARL SANDBURG HAS RETURNED TO THE SOIL HE LOVED.
>
> THE ASHES OF THE LATE POET AND AUTHOR OF GREAT MAGNITUDE WERE SCATTERED IN THE SHADOW OF A HUGE GRANITE BOULDER CALLED REMEMBRANCE ROCK IN A 1½-ACRE PARK HERE, BEHIND THE THREE-ROOM COTTAGE THAT WAS HIS BOYHOOD HOME.
>
> ILLINOIS GOV. OTTO KERNER PRESIDED AT A MEMORIAL SERVICE SUNDAY, COMMEMORATING THE PRIVATE CEREMONY AT DUSK SATURDAY. "THEY WILL REMAIN HERE ALWAYS IN THE AREA HE LOVED VERY, VERY MUCH," KERNER TOLD A CROWD OF 2,500.
>
> AS HE SPOKE, TRAINS ROARED DOWN NEARBY TRACKS, REMINDING THOSE PAYING HOMAGE OF HIS DAYS RIDING THE RAILS, GATHERING MATERIAL TO WEAVE HIS PROSE AND POETRY.

In four short paragraphs we are given a torrent of specific detail—the acreage of the park, the kind of stone of which Remembrance Rock is composed, the number of rooms in Sandburg's boyhood home, the time of day the private services were held, the number of people attending the services at which the governor spoke the next day. No mention is made of Sandburg's Lincoln writings, for which he is best known. The phrase "author of great magnitude" is unfortunate. In the last sentence, confusing use is made of the pronouns *he* and *his*.

Let's say a news writer has this piece of wire copy and is told to boil it down to twenty-five seconds—all the time available for it in a broadcast that goes on the air in ten minutes. This presents the writer with a real problem. To "tell" the story so that the broadcaster can read it in twenty-five seconds, he must cut the wire service version of what happened almost in half. He decides at once to skip the reference to Remembrance Rock. He feels that if he mentions it, he must say that Sandburg once wrote a book by the same name. There's not time for that kind of background. He also decides to concentrate on what happened today—Sunday. What happened Saturday is yesterday's news. He leaves out a lot of other detail, and five minutes before air time he's finished. The story, condensed for broadcast, reads:

> The ashes of Carl Sandburg have been returned to the soil of his hometown—Galesburg, Illinois. At a memorial service today, Governor Kerner said, "They will remain here always, in the area he loved very, very much." As the governor spoke, trains could be heard passing

through, reminding the crowd of the days . . . long ago . . . when the poet and Lincoln biographer was poor and rode the rails.

Some factual information has been sacrificed. But is the listener really cheated? Will he miss not knowing the acreage of the park or any of the other details that have been dropped? Listeners who want these details know they will find them in the print media.

You will notice that mention is made in the broadcast version of Sandburg's role as Lincoln biographer. And, of course, reference is made to Galesburg, Illinois— something the UPI writer didn't have to do because of the dateline on the story, although *dateline* is now a vestigial term so far as wire services are concerned. They no longer give the date in their datelines, only the place.

Sometimes—too often for comfort—you will write a story and discover it runs too long. You must cut. It means killing words, phrases, perhaps whole sentences which you believed, when you wrote them, were absolutely essential.

Beware of long sentences. When Ed Bradley was asked to introduce the winners of the duPont–Columbia Awards, he was supplied with a script that began

Good evening and welcome, everyone, to the Alfred I. duPont–Columbia University Awards that have come to be regarded as the highest in broadcast journalism.

A veteran broadcaster, Bradley recognized the need to break up the 23-word sentence. He did it by saying:

Good evening and welcome, everyone, to the Alfred I. duPont–Columbia University Awards, the awards that have come to be regarded as the highest in broadcast journalism.

By breaking the sentence in the middle, he not only made it easier to read but more readily understood. He was giving his audience one fact at a time.

For years, at the end of each year, Charles Kuralt has recalled the famous who died during that year. On the "Sunday Morning" broadcast of December 29, 1991, he noted the passing of the likes of Frank Capra, Rudolf Serkin, Ralph Bellamy, and Eva Le Gallienne, and sixty others. Of these, six were journalists. He said over their pictures:

Homer Bigart was a legend in journalism long before he died this year. The newspaperman's newspaperman, the best. When his editors gave Homer Bigart a big story and a deadline, what they got back from him a couple hours later was, often as not, literature. Alexander Kendrick was another user of the language. He spoke history into CBS News, as did Peter Kalischer, as did Doug Kiker of NBC. If those good reporters had not been born, there would be gaps now in the chronicle of our times.

Television turned John Daly, urbane newsman, into John Daly, urbane game show host. Everybody liked John Daly. And Harry Reasoner. The remarkable thing about Harry Reasoner is that television did not change him, not at all. Oh, Harry, if you had not been born, half of all the wry and graceful reporting there ever was on these airwaves would have been something else entirely. How odd that it should be so easy to forget all those who clamored for attention, but impossible to forget this one who did not. We could not have done without even one of those who died this year.

Only with such succinctness can sixty-four obituaries be compressed into a few minutes. Only with skill can it be done with such grace.

The Tease

The tease comes in four styles. They all require tight writing, and we shall take up each in the order they normally appear.

First, there is the tease for a story coming up later in the day, such as "Latest on the subway strike at ten." Marvin Kitman, TV critic for *Newsday,* says some teases are supposed to stop you dead in your tracks, such as "Poisoned food in your refrigerator at eleven!" Such teases are always terse. Usually they have no verb. The story they promote is the story the producer believes most likely to attract viewers.

Next is the tease that appears as a news summary at the top of a half-hour or one-hour newscast—the "headlines tease." This tease goes back to the early days of radio. It was also used when Walter Cronkite went on the air in 1963 with network television's first half-hour evening news. The trick then, as now, is to highlight the news of the day without really reporting it. For example, instead of saying that both sides in a postal workers strike have agreed to go back to the bargaining table, the sentence might read "The postal strike takes a new turn." If stories were summarized in a way that satisfied viewers' curiosity about what happened, some would turn to another channel or switch off their sets.

Within a newscast, the anchor may tease a story coming up in the next segment—the "stay-tuned tease." For example, this tease was used by Dan Rather: "Coming up, the story of how George Steinbrenner, the New York Yankees owner, may be put out at home." The story concerned possible disciplining of Steinbrenner for alleged payment of forty thousand dollars to a self-described gambler. Note the metaphor in "put out at home." Creativity on the part of a writer is shown in this tease for an upcoming story on Christmas shopping: "Is there a pall on the mall as holiday shoppers think small? The answer in a moment."

Nice touch, but don't try so hard for effect that you end up looking foolish, as did the anchor who teased, "Recession bangs home for thousands of workers." It's good the writer wanted a strong verb, but this one, with all its muscle, misses the mark. And you don't always have to be creative. Occasionally, to save time, Peter Jennings will say simply, "We'll be back in just a moment."

Finally, there's the visual tease that appears, often in block letters, just before a commercial. It looks like this:

STORM OVER
COURT RULING

These teases are bare bones, yet they entice. Sometimes they amuse, as did this tease for the report by ABC's Charles Murphy on a stock show where cows were treated as queens, if only for a day:

COW BELLES

We said there are four kinds of teases. However, Kitman has deplored a fifth, which he calls "the slease tease." Here are two examples, the first from Channel 2 in Chicago, and the second from Channel 5 in San Francisco: "A rash of rapes on the campus of Northwestern!" and "Public lives, private pain. The illnesses that afflict your favorite celebrities."

This is tabloid journalism. We wish we could say you never will have to write stuff like that. But you may, especially in sweeps periods when your station's audience is being measured.

The Good Word

As suggested earlier, one way to keep your writing tight is to use the good short word that says the same thing as a long word or even a whole phrase.

For a minute, let your teacher be Ed Murrow. Here is some of his actual editing. First, the sentence as originally written, then Murrow's revision:

Mao Tse-tung has *relinquished* one of his top posts.
Mao Tse-tung has *given up* one of his top posts.

The message came *prior to his departure*.
The message came *before he left*.

The Justice Department contends that his naturalization was obtained *fraudulently*.
The Justice Department contends that his naturalization was obtained *by fraud*.

They acted because of an *anticipated* increase.
They acted because of an *expected* increase.

Mr. Eisenhower *reiterated* his proposal for "open skies" inspection.
Mr. Eisenhower *repeated* his proposal for "open skies" inspection.

In the interim, he has waged a *protracted* legal battle.
In the interim, he has waged a *long* legal battle.

Murrow edited his copy to make it tighter, more readable, more direct. Some of the words he shunned are what H. W. Fowler in his *Dictionary of Modern English Usage* calls "stylish" words. It's a mistake, Fowler says, to think you can improve your style by using these words—the effect is apt to be pretentious. Among the "stylish" words listed by Fowler are: *assist* (for *help*), *beverage* (for *drink*), *category* (for *class*), *commence* (for *begin*), and *sufficient* (for *enough*).

The phrase *very unique* is both overstuffed and embarrassing. Just say *unique*. What's unique is one of a kind. Fowler says only the illiterate confuse it with adjectives like *exceptional* and *rare*.

Excess syllables represent waste. Often you can save time by using:

act for *take action*	*false* for *spurious*
ask for *question*	*first* for *initial*
basic for *elementary*	*home* for *residence*
beat for *defeat*	*hurt* for *injure*
big for *prodigious*	*long* for *lengthy*
bill for *measure*	*measure* for *legislation*
buy for *purchase*	*often* for *frequently*
car for *vehicle*	*on* for *upon*
cost for *expense*	*rebuke* for *reprimand*
cuts and bruises for	*send* for *transmit*
lacerations and abrasions	*speech* for *address*
*start** for *begin*	*sure* for *certain*
each for *every*	*take part* for *participate*
end for *conclude*	*try* for *attempt* or *endeavor*
expense for *expenditure*	*urge* for *persuade*

More is involved than saving time. The fewer syllables you use, the clearer, cleaner, stronger the sentences you write.

If possible, go for the one-syllable word. One-syllable words are high octane. Don't let their simplicity fool you; while contributing to clarity, they give your sentences added power.

Doubt it? Listen to some of them: *win, lose, live, die, help, hold, hurt, save, kill, joy, trust, love, hate, truth, hope.* And then there are all the so-called four-letter words that endure for their shock value. Short words that endure because they are strong. Richard Lederer, an authority on words, said, "Short words are bright like

*A famous TV director used to say, "Let's commence to begin!"

sparks that glow in the night, prompt like the dawn that greets the day, sharp like the blade of a knife.''

All short words.

When Emerson Stone was CBS's vice president of news for radio, he picked out some choice examples of wordy writing. Here they are, along with the comments he made in a memorandum to his staff:

General consensus. *Consensus* carries the meaning of a meeting of minds.
General is superfluous.
The aim of the move was intended to discourage waste. Why not drop *the aim of?*
From whence they came. *Whence* incorporates the meaning of *from*, which therefore can be dropped.
The reason for this, according to Young, is because. . . . Make it, ''The reason, according to Young, is that. . . .'' *Because* is redundant. You don't need *for this*.
He said he allegedly has a witness. Why *allegedly?*
Besides this action, the baseball owners must also decide. . . . *Besides this action* is superfluous.
Thousands have been killed and tens of thousands more are starving. *More* is redundant.
But the true facts came out. Forget *true*. A rose is a rose is a rose. Pigs is pigs, and facts is facts.

We have found these other examples of words wasted in broadcast scripts by using

at this point in time for *now*
do injury to for *injure*
due to the fact that for *because*
in an effort to for *to*
in order to for *to*
is capable of for *can*
make changes in for *change*
prior to for *before*
provide proof for *prove*
sounded their praise for *praised*
took that walk down the aisle for *married*
will be able to for *can*
would be able to for *could*

There is a debate over the use of *whether or not*. While print journalists, quite correctly, find the *or not* superfluous, there are occasions in writing news for broadcast when the full phrase serves a useful purpose. That purpose is emphasis. Example:

> Negotiations in the next few hours will determine whether or not subway trains in New York City will be running tomorrow.

Here, *or not* makes a contribution. The two small words magnify for the listener—dramatize, if you will—the alternatives: Will the subways run, or will they be shut down? Moreover, by employing the whole phrase *whether or not,* the writer has given the broadcaster, like the actor in a play, an opportunity to underscore the alternatives further by his reading of the line. Always remember that as you write for ear, you also are writing for voice.

Words can be saved in reporting a running story. A devastating hurricane may have been in the news only twenty-four hours, but since every newscast and every daily newspaper in the country will have been reporting the storm's progress, it can be assumed that the listener knows of its existence, though obviously there are always a few listeners who have been out of touch. But even the listener who has not heard of the storm understands if you say

> *That* off-season hurricane has struck Havana, killing at least 50 people. Damage is estimated in the hundreds of millions of dollars.

Two other examples:

> All passengers have been rescued from *that* cruise ship sinking off the coast of Portugal.
>
> Doctors report that two of *those* quintuplets born yesterday in Mexico City have died.

Again, the device of using *that* and *those* enables the newscaster to get to the heart of what is new in the story in the fewest possible words.

Where Loss Equals Gain

If the first commandment in broadcast style is to be conversational, the second commandment is to be concise. In his introduction to William Strunk Jr.'s marvelous little book on the elements of style, E. B. White tells how Professor Strunk taught the art of pruning language to make it more effective. White said: "The student learns to cut the deadwood from 'this is a subject that,' reducing it to 'this subject,' a saving of three words. He learns to trim 'used for fuel purposes' down to 'used for fuel.' He learns that he is being a chatterbox when he says 'the question as to whether' and that he should just say 'whether'—a gain of four words out of a possible five."

Note that White equates the elimination—loss—of unnecessary words with *gain.*

Each word should work for you. A nonworking word reduces clarity, fogs up what you are trying to say, and should be cast off. In broadcast journalism, conciseness carries a double premium. Not only is concise language more effective, making for clarity, but it also saves time. And time is the "container" in which news items—visuals and script—are packaged. The more concisely, cleanly the stories are written, the more room to report items which otherwise would be left out.

Almost every newscast, regardless of length, is a "tight show" if you are trying conscientiously to report the most important, most interesting developments of the day. If it is a light day and not much has happened, you can use the extra room to explain, perhaps through background, more of the significance of what did happen. When the television networks expanded their evening news programs to a half-hour, they wondered if there would be trouble filling the time. That problem never arose. The problem the producers face is the old one: how best to report the news in the time available to them.

8. *The Time Element*

Broadcasting is the "now" medium. Radio and television can report what is happening right now, or what has just happened. Or, for that matter, what is just about to happen. For this reason, the present, perfect, and future tenses are used more than in print journalism. The past tense is used much less. The late Allan Jackson of CBS was an authority on broadcast writing. He said: "Just because newspapers and wire associations write everything in the past tense doesn't mean that we on the electronic side of the business must, or even should, follow suit. Nothing sounds sillier than to hear some broadcaster say something to the effect that 'John Doe said he *thought* Christmas was a good idea.' Doesn't he still think so?"

There are times when it is best to use the past tense. If you use the past tense in a lead, you should include the time element.

The Senate voted *today* to reform the income tax program.

You could, of course, say "this afternoon" or "tonight," if either of these apply. In fact, in an evening broadcast use *tonight* whenever you truthfully can. It makes the news sound fresher. In any case, if you use the past tense in a lead, tell when.

An exception would be if you are wrapping together several related stories. If you report the Senate action on tax reform, and then go on to report House passage of an anti-crime measure and conference committee agreement on a public housing bill, there's no need to add the time element to the last two stories. It is taken for granted by the listener, after hearing the first story, that these other congressional actions also took place today. Thus, the leads to the three stories, reported in succession, might read:

> The Senate voted today to reform the income tax program.
>
> The House approved the controversial anti-crime bill.
>
> And a Senate-House committee agreed on a measure to provide public housing for 200-thousand low-income families.

No need in these last two stories to use *today*. It's assumed.

You would not have had to use the past tense in reporting any of these stories. "The Senate has voted to reform the income tax program" is every bit as good a lead as "The Senate voted today to reform the income tax program." But, as we said, if you do choose to use the past tense, you need the adverb *today* or its equivalent.

Avoid a succession of leads containing the word *today*, especially in news summaries when repetition of the word becomes painful. Vary the tenses of your leads. Use the present and perfect tenses when they are appropriate. Your newscast "listens" better if you do this, and you are exploiting the fact that broadcast news is what is happening now. It is not only a natural, correct way to report the news but the most interesting way from the point of view of the listener, who is impressed by the immediacy of what you are reporting. The listener enjoys it.

You will enjoy it, too. Within minutes after a bulletin moves on the wire—sometimes within seconds—you have shared the news with a vast audience. There is excitement in writing a present-tense lead like

> The FBI is holding eight men accused of plotting to blow up the United Nations headquarters in New York.

Reflect the swiftness of the medium in what you write. For example:

> At this moment, the United States Navy is carrying out a missile attack against Iraq in response to its attempt to assassinate former President Bush.

So here is another tip on tenses. You are reporting news that is *new*. Let it sound that way. Don't hide it!

The present tense is by no means restricted to such bulletin-like material. It can—and should—be used in such relatively routine stories as

> The President is flying to Chicago, where tonight he will make a major foreign policy speech.

Here you can say "is flying" because the President has taken off from Andrews Air Force Base and actually is in the air, flying to Chicago. A newspaper or wire service can't say that. By the time the press reporter's story is published and reaches the reader, the President will already have arrived in Chicago. Chances are, he will also have given his speech.

Here's an example of effective use of the perfect tense in a lead:

> Congress has just recessed.

The listener is being told what just happened, and he knows it. Another reason for using the perfect tense is that we use it so often in everyday speech. Note how ''natural'' these leads sound:

> Rescue workers in Mississippi have found the bodies of 100 more victims of yesterday's hurricane.
>
> The Chinese have test-fired a new version of the Scud missile.
>
> Those peace talks in Geneva have ended.

Avoid a succession of perfect tenses in the same sentence. It has an awkward sound. For example, do not write

> The White House has announced that President Clinton has decided against going to Europe at this time.

Instead, write

> The White House announces that President Clinton has decided against going to Europe at this time.

Do not ''gild the lily'' by adding *today* when you have used the perfect tense. Do not say

> The Senate today has passed a new civil rights bill.

Say either

> The Senate passed a new civil rights bill today.

or

> The Senate has passed a new civil rights bill.

Choose one or the other, not both.

In some leads, no verb—hence, no tense—is used at all. More about leads later.

Don't Cheat

Don't say ''today'' when the story broke yesterday. Such practice can prove embarrassing (viewers may have heard the story the preceding day), and it is inaccurate.

Be resourceful. Update the story. Move it into the present by highlighting a new fact you may find through a telephone call or discover buried in the last paragraph of the story that moved on the wire. Don't start your story by saying, "A truce was agreed upon yesterday by the warring factions in Croatia," even if you have nothing new to report. If there's no word of the truce being broken, say so. But don't start with yesterday's lead. If you do, you are proclaiming to your listeners that all you have is stale news. (And while you are at it, get rid of the passive voice.)

It is perfectly proper to conceal the time someone said something, or something occurred, if the time element is not of consequence. Example: If in mid-morning you are reporting what the President did the preceding night, it is not necessary to say:

> Last night, President Clinton outlined his economic program to the country.

It is no violation of journalistic principle, in this instance, to leave out the time element so that the story reads:

> President Clinton has outlined his economic program to the country.

What is newsworthy here is that the president had finally spelled out his program. But we should emphasize that in some stories the time element is significant and must be reported. The listener must be told that something happened "yesterday" or "last night" whenever omission of that fact distorts the story or robs it of meaning.

Unnatural Usage

In many wire service stories the time element is brought in unnaturally by the scruff of the neck. Example:

> QUICK ACTION BY PRISON GUARDS AVERTED WEDNESDAY A THREATENED RACE RIOT IN THE WALLED YARD OF SAN QUENTIN PRISON.

The guards didn't avert Wednesday. They averted a threatened race riot. In normal conversation, you would never place the noun *Wednesday* immediately after the transitive verb *averted*. And you wouldn't say *Wednesday*. You would say *today*. In a newscast, the story might start out simply:

> A race riot was averted today at San Quentin prison.

It should be observed, because so much broadcast copy is rewritten from the wires, that both the Associated Press and United Press International regularly use the name of the day of the week instead of *today* in their night leads. This is in keeping with the special requirements of the print media. The writer of broadcast news should stay with *today,* and, contrary to the wire services, should use the words *yesterday* and *tomorrow.* It is confusing to a person listening to the news on Friday to be told that something happened on Thursday or will happen on Saturday. He has to say to himself, "Oh, yes. Today is Friday."

The good professional writer avoids words the listener must translate.

What Time Is It?

The time element can cause trouble in other ways. A major newscaster was embarrassed on the air when, in introducing a video report by a correspondent in Prague, he said that it was on the night of August 20, 1968, that Russian troops invaded Czechoslovakia. The correspondent, in his report, said that the Russian invasion occurred on August 21, 1968. They were both right. It was on the night of August 20, New York time, and on August 21, Prague time. But such contradictions in script, obviously, are to be avoided. The writer, having previewed the report, should have known the date used by the correspondent and not mentioned it in his introduction. He could, in short, have written around it, avoiding the contradiction.

Pay particular attention to the time element in stories from the Far East. A wire service story is written in local time. That is, in the time of the place where the story originates. When something happened in China on Wednesday, Beijing time, it may have happened on Tuesday, New York time. If the story reports that a statement was issued in Beijing on Wednesday night, the writer of a script for broadcast in New York cannot on Wednesday night, New York time, say, "The statement was issued tonight." Not only is the word *tonight* inaccurate, it makes the broadcaster look foolish because, due to the time difference, listeners to other news programs have been hearing about the statement all during the day. "How," the listener asks, "can the statement have been issued tonight when I heard it reported on that other station this morning?"

Here is an example of carelessness, or deception, in the reporting a story from the Middle East. Menachem Begin, the former prime minister of Israel, died at 3:30 A.M., March 9, 1992, Tel Aviv time. That was 9:30 P.M., March 8, New York time. The news was reported that night on radio and television stations throughout the United States. The next day other stations and at least one major network, instead of reporting that Begin had died "last night," said he died "today." This may have been deliberate falsification in order to "freshen up" the story; if so, that was deceit. When listeners hear the word *today,* they naturally assume the speaker is referring to that day in America, not in some other part of the world.

So, don't fudge on the time element to "freshen" your story because: (1) it's wrong, and (2) you will be found out.

The Midnight Writer

For the writer of "The Midnight News" the time element offers a special problem. If, for example, it is midnight Saturday, the news actually will be heard during the first few minutes of Sunday. How do you, writing at midnight, refer to an event that occurred earlier in the evening? Do you say it occurred last night? And how do you refer to what happened Saturday and what will happen Sunday or Monday?

In the first instance, you would technically be right in saying "last night." It already is Sunday. But in the minds of many listeners it still is Saturday night. The phrase *last night* will confuse them. For the same reason, they will be confused by references to "yesterday," "today," and "tomorrow."

What's the answer?

Probably the best way is to use, whenever possible, the present and perfect tenses without reference to the day. If mention of the specific day is required, say "Saturday," "Sunday," or "Monday." Also, *Saturday night* is preferable to *last night*. It is awkward, but still the best solution. (In writing the troublesome midnight news, some writers simply use *tonight,* and that seems to work.)

The Advance Text

Be scrupulous in observing the release time on stories. But frequently a dinner speech to be delivered at eight or nine o'clock in the evening, local time, will be marked for release at 6:30 P.M. This is because the speaker, or the organization he is addressing, wants to "make" the networks' early evening news. The result is that you will be reporting the speech before it is ever made.

How do you write this? Can you report that the speaker said something which he has not yet said?

The answer is that you can't. You *can* say "in a speech John Brown *is going to give* later tonight," or "John Brown says, in the advance text of a speech he *will give* later tonight," or, "according to the advance we have of a speech John Brown *is making* tonight," or, "in a speech he *is scheduled to give* tonight." Speakers often change their speeches at the last minute. You are leveling with listeners when you let them know you are quoting from an advance text. It takes you off the hook if the speaker does not say what you say he's going to say.

We have taken a dinner speech as an example. Of course, the same kind of treatment should be given to any speech, the text of which is released in advance.

9. *The Lead*

The lead is the most important line in any story. It should be clear. It should entice. It should set the tone. But since a lead can also confuse or be a turn-off, they must be written with care. Because many of the best leads contain few words, those words must be well chosen.

One of the more memorable pictures captured for television was that of President Bush's collapse at a Japanese state dinner on January 8, 1992. The President had gone to Tokyo to negotiate agreements that would help American automakers. Stories written less than a day later for the *Washington Post* and the television networks show plainly the difference between broadcast writing and the less conversational, more complicated writing for print.

Here is the lead, datelined Tokyo, that appeared in the *Washington Post:*

> President Bush, looking cheerful but drawn and tired, emerged this afternoon nearly a day after he vomited, collapsed to the floor from his chair and was forced to leave an official dinner suffering what his physicians said was intestinal flu as he neared the end of his 12-day, four-nation Pacific tour.

This sentence runs much too long for a newscast—fifty-two words. And it is crammed with too much information. If you heard it, you wouldn't—couldn't—absorb it. Remember, if a sentence, any sentence, you write runs more than 20 words, test it for clarity. Chances are you can write a cleaner, simpler sentence that's more readily understood. And often if it's leaner—stripped down—it's also stronger.

The lead Peter Jennings used on ABC's ''World News Tonight'' contrasts sharply with the lead in the *Washington Post.*

We begin, of course, with the President's health. On the other side of the international dateline, in Tokyo, the President is up and around. In fact, he's been speaking to the Vice President, Dan Quayle. Not too very long ago, he told the Vice President he was indeed up and around and, in the President's words, "feeling great." We may be getting further news from the White House spokesman in the next few minutes. But it was quite a scare only 12 hours ago—20 minutes past eight in the evening, Tokyo time, in the middle of yet another official dinner—when Mr. Bush collapsed. Here's our White House correspondent, Brit Hume.

While the *Post* masses fifty-two words in its first sentence, Jennings uses eight. In his next sentence he gives the answer to the question uppermost in viewers' minds: The president is all right. Then in another short sentence he reveals that Bush has been talking by telephone with Dan Quayle. And so on, short sentence after short sentence, until he switches to Brit Hume.

The immediacy of broadcast news is demonstrated when Jennings says there may be further word on the president's condition "in the next few minutes." It's an immediacy—a sense of "this is a breaking story, and we're on top of it"—that newspapers cannot match.

Dan Rather's CBS lead is more dramatic:

It was a frightening picture, the President of the United States collapsed under a banquet table in Tokyo, ashen-faced, barely conscious, if indeed he was conscious, for a few seconds. But it's now the morning after in Japan, and official spokesmen say Mr. Bush is recovering from a bout of stomach flu and is expected to resume much of his schedule. Correspondent Randall Pinkston begins our coverage of the President's health.

Like Jennings, Rather makes the president's health the heart of the story. But he starts with the drama, "the frightening picture." Videotape of the stricken president will be shown, but up front, in their minds, viewers see the president of the United States collapsed under a table, "ashen-faced, barely conscious."

At NBC, Tom Brokaw takes a less graphic approach.

It's a new day in Japan, and it should be a better one for George Bush, now that he's had a night's rest and treatment for intestinal flu. His collapse at a state dinner was a frightening scene, but his doctors and aides insist the President's condition is not serious. NBC's John Cochran is on the watch for us tonight in Tokyo. John?

While Rather starts with what happened and Jennings with what is happening as he goes on the air, Brokaw anticipates what will happen. He foresees a better day for the President, now that he had received treatment.

These broadcast leads are conversational, and note the simplicity with which they start.

> "We begin, of course, with the President's health."
> "It was a frightening picture. . . ."
> "It's a new day in Japan. . . ."

There is instruction in these beginnings. They set up the story, but don't hit you right off with details.

No doubt you will find in these leads more to discuss. Brokaw refers to intestinal flu, Rather to stomach flu. Is it possible Rather shied away from the adjective *intestinal* because he was being heard at mealtime? Does it matter? What is there about these leads that makes them conversational? Do you see any way they could have been improved? And which broadcast lead do you like the best? Why?

The Verbless Lead

A lead may be written without a verb. The practice is fairly common in broadcast news. This style is appropriate because it is both conversational and brief, such as "A surprise today from the Supreme Court." Here are some other examples.

> "Another teachers strike, this one in New York."
> "A close call in the air over Boston."
> "A familiar issue today in Congress."

And this delightful one referring to the faulty space telescope: "More trouble with Hubble."

Besides being brief, the verbless lead also makes for a change of pace. But, because it would sound awkward, a succession of verbless leads should be avoided.

"Umbrellas"

Most broadcast leads emphasize a single development: "The city's school system has run out of money." Other leads encompass several related developments. This summary lead is often called an "umbrella" lead and can be effective in stories with multiple angles or developments. Examples:

> "A series of tornadoes hit the Southwest overnight."
> "There was a burst of activity today on Capitol Hill."

The umbrella lead covers several developments which have something in common. In January 1991, when much of the Midwest was hit by a series of winter storms, Tom Brokaw's lead on NBC was "In the Midwest, it was winter with a vengeance."

An umbrella lead should not be used toward the end of any newscast that hasn't been carefully timed. You can't report "a series of winter storms" and then mention only one before you run out of time. Individual items reported under such an umbrella should be brief, if you expect your listener to carry the sense of the lead throughout the story. For the same reason, if the lead says there are two major developments in a story, you should at least introduce your listeners to what those are before describing the first of the two in some detail.

Don't try to force umbrella leads. They will come naturally if the items introduced belong together.

The Set-up Line

It is especially difficult to write a good lead when there are a lot of angles to a story. Leads that try to combine all, or most, of the elements in a complex story are bound to be confusing. The trick, when confronted with that kind of story, is to use what is often called the "set-up line." This is a line that introduces the story, cues it effectively, interestingly, and honestly, but makes no attempt to go into detail. Here are some set-up lines:

> "Things have gone from bad to worse in Haiti."
> "There are new complications in the budget bill."
> "The Governor has suggested a number of possible solutions to Miami's crime problem."

The strategy is obvious. You generalize, then go to the specifics. After the set-up line you can report, piecemeal, the problems in Haiti or the complications in the budget bill. Following the lead about the Governor's suggested solutions, you would describe some, or all, of them, one-by-one.

The set-up line is a close cousin of the umbrella lead. The difference is that while the umbrella covers a series of related stories—stories with a common denominator—the set-up line is useful in introducing a single story that poses a problem because it has several elements.

The Five W's and H

Generations of journalists have summarized their six basic questions as the "five W's and H." As indicated earlier, few newspapers still insist on beginning a story by telling "who, what, where, when, why, and how"—all in one sentence. Some editors advise their reporters to answer the five W's and H in the lead but say the lead may encompass several sentences. This compromise with tradition clearly comes from a desire to make newspapers easier to read and understand.

Good broadcast leads typically include the more descriptive of these six categories—where, when, who, and what. It is difficult to cite good broadcast leads that involve the other two categories—how and why. Here are leads used by Ed Murrow exemplifying the four descriptive categories:

Where: I'm standing again tonight on a rooftop looking out over London, feeling rather large and lonesome.

When: Early this morning we heard the bombers going out. It was the sound of a giant factory in the sky.

Who: General Eisenhower finished speaking in Abilene about 15 minutes ago.

What: There are no words to describe the thing that is happening. Today I talked with eight American correspondents in London. Six of them had been forced to move. All had stories of bombs, and all agreed that they were unable to convey through print or spoken word an accurate impression of what's happening in London these days and nights.

It was Murrow's habit to get to the point immediately. He rarely began with the how or why, but dealt with those aspects in the body of his report. Attempts to use the how or why in a lead will usually result in more bad writing than good. Witness this example:

In view of the continuing budget deficit, the President today stressed the need to reduce spending.

We wouldn't *say* that. In conversation we don't start sentences with long prepositional phrases, so don't write that way. Start with the "what" instead of the "why."

The President today stressed the need to reduce spending in view of the continuing budget deficit.

Now you have the horse before the cart. You also have the cart-horse relationship correct in this version, further improved, if you say:

The President today stressed the need to reduce spending. This is necessary, he said, in view of the continuing budget deficit.

There seldom is only *one* correct way to write a story. The test in each case is: Is it effective? Is it clear? Remember, always, that you are in the business of communicating.

You will inevitably report votes taken by legislative bodies. Don't say

By a vote of six to three, the City Council today killed the mayor's downtown parking plan.

This isn't good because the listener is getting the results of a vote before knowing who voted or what the voting was about. Far better is

> The City Council today killed the mayor's downtown parking plan. The vote was six to three.

You have now provided your listeners with a frame of reference. They know what the vote was about. You have also done something else. You have gotten more quickly to the substance of the story, and you have separated the elements of the story and given them to your listeners, one at a time. Throughout the lead, what happened is absolutely clear.

(Note: If a vote is taken on a measure, say a crucial appropriations bill in the U.S. Senate, and the bill is passed by a vote of 97 to 1, it is important to identify the lone dissenter. Your listeners will certainly be wondering who the die-hard senator was, so you must tell them. Similarly, you shouldn't say in a lead that the Senate approved two amendments to a space exploration bill and then report on only one of the amendments. It's a mistake to sprinkle a script with unanswered questions.)

Unfamiliar names may be missed unless your listeners are prepared for them. As we said earlier, they need to be "teed up"—put into place before being spoken. If the person's name is a real jawbreaker, leave it out of your lead sentence. Instead of

> The premier of Iceland, Bjarni Benediktsson, died today in a fire that also claimed the life of his wife and one of their grandchildren.

say

> The premier of Iceland died today in a fire that also claimed the life of his wife and one of their grandchildren. Bjarni Benediktsson had been premier for seven years.

Then tell about the fire and give whatever other information, such as the premier's age, the story warrants.

Try to remember that starting a lead sentence—or any sentence for that matter—with a long dependent clause or phrase is not good. "In the wake of a record-breaking cold snap that has caused an undetermined amount of damage to the Florida citrus crop, an increase in fruit prices is expected." That's a "crawfish" lead. Crawfish like to travel backward. Get the substance of your story out there—in front. In this instance, the writer should have started with the expected increase in the price of fruit.

Some broadcast newswriters, when faced with a series of short items, like to start them with phrases like "In London," "In Tokyo," or "Here in Washington." These phrases serve as datelines. They establish immediately where the event being reported took place. The listener is oriented. Prepared. This device is also helpful in another, less obvious, way. When the place name is given at the head of the lead sentence, the rest of the lead is easier to write. This is because after a phrase like "In London today," you have a simpler task. You have disposed of the business of where the thing happened and when it happened. Now all you have to do is report what happened.

The best leads are written by reporters who are creative. Here's an example: On Christmas Day 1992, Charlayne Hunter-Gault is reporting from Somalia for the MacNeil/Lehrer NewsHour. As the report begins, viewers see a little makeshift Christmas tree. It looks forlorn, and Hunter-Gault says:

> It was a Christmas tree like no other, put up by American troops near the airport tarmac in Baidoa for a Christmas like no other in a land where Christmas never comes.

She goes on to explain that most Somalis are Muslim and that this is the first sign of Christmas she has seen in Somalia. Then she reports what is happening. The lead is lovely. It is simple. With its rhythmic flow of sound, it approaches poetry and creates just the right mood.

Try, without exaggerating or lapsing into bad taste, to make your leads interesting. Be original. Think, always, how you could make it better. Recall Tom Brokaw's lead "In the Midwest, it was winter with a vengeance." That is considerably more interesting than if the lead had been "The worst winter storm in Michigan since 1982 dumped nine inches of snow on Detroit, closing the airport and stopping rush hour traffic. The storm also hit parts of Ohio and Indiana."

When the FBI reported a decrease in major crime but an increase in less serious crime, Joseph Dembo of CBS lifted the story from the ordinary when he wrote "This year Americans are killing each other less and stealing from each other more." On the CBS evening news, Connie Chung used this lead: "The first international study of smoking and women was out today, and it's a killer."

It's important not to strain too hard, as in this instance: "The import of Chinese assault rifles has shot up." If you are going to play with words—make a pun—be sure it comes off. This one fizzled. For a serious subject, it was too cute.

On a small New England station a reporter said, "It looks like forced busing will come to Newburyport." No doubt this caught listeners' attention. But it was wrong. What the story really was about was the lack of train service to Boston, which meant that more Newburyport commuters would have to take buses. The writer, striving to be creative, misled listeners for whom the phrase *forced busing* had special meaning. Also, for good grammar, the reporter should have used *as though* instead of *like*.

Although good writers usually try to simplify complex stories, you can mislead by oversimplifying. You want your lead to be simple. Uncomplicated. You want to grab attention. But if you are responsible, you also want the meaning—the true meaning—to be clear. So even if it complicates your lead, or even weakens it a bit, leave in the qualifiers. If something is reported to have happened, and you have any doubt that it actually has happened, label it for what it is—a report. And say who reported it, though not necessarily in the first sentence. If something is almost done, or almost decided, do not say in your lead that it is done or decided. It does no good to distort the lead and add the qualifier later in the story. If you do that, you are saying, in effect, "I misled you. I played a little game with you. Actually, it hasn't quite been done or decided yet."

In leads, don't *mis*lead. It is not the way to build an audience. Or trust.

Who Said That?

Attributions must precede quoted material on radio and television. A wire service story might go like this:

WASHINGTON—THE CLINTON ADMINISTRATION WILL SUPPORT EDUCATORS ADVOCATING A SINGLE SET OF PERFORMANCE STANDARDS FOR PUBLIC SCHOOLS, WHITE HOUSE SOURCES SAID TODAY.

The problem with this attribution is that it dangles. For broadcast you put it at the head of the sentence:

White House sources say the Clinton Administration will support those educators advocating a single set of performance standards for public schools.

Now listeners know who is making the prediction at the time they hear it. Moreover, the style is conversational. It's more like what you would say.

It is especially important that attributions accompany all statements that imply blame, are of doubtful validity, or that may be disputed. As stressed in Chapter 4, first reports of disasters normally need attribution. Who said the airliner crashed? Who said there was an earthquake? When corroborating reports remove doubt, drop the attribution. But you need to cite a source in any investigative follow-up that fixes blame.

Attribution is especially important in crime reporting. In the streamlining process central to broadcast newswriting, there is danger that necessary attribution may be dropped. Remember that an accused person is just that—accused—until proved guilty in a court of law.

Conscience and common sense should be the writer's guide for using attribution. The story is told that when Mark Twain was a reporter, his editor instructed, "Never state anything as fact that you do not know of your own personal knowledge." The next day Twain submitted: "A woman giving the name of Mrs. James Jones, who is reported to be one of the society leaders of this city, is said to have given what is purported to be a party yesterday to a number of alleged ladies. The hostess claims to be the wife of a reputed lawyer.''

Even so, proper attribution is no joke.

Setting the Tone

A good lead sets the tone of the story, preparing the listener for what you're about to tell. On October 11, 1991, Jeff Greenfield of ABC News drew the assignment to summarize the testimony before the Senate Judiciary Committee regarding charges of sexual harassment brought against Supreme Court nominee Judge Clarence Thomas by Professor Anita Hill. Greenfield's simple, effective lead was ''There has never been a day like this on Capitol Hill.''

Be alert to times when the content of the story can help set the tone for the lead. As the financial troubles of Pan American Airlines were mounting, a CBS newscast led with ''Pan Am has flown into turbulence.''

A few months later, when Pan Am announced it was going out of business, Dan Rather led the CBS evening news with ''It's the end of the runway for Pan American, a pioneer in commercial aviation.'' Simple and direct. Just the right touch. Another appropriate play on words in a serious story was used by Dan Rather in reporting the financial problems of a well-known New York department store: ''Macy's paraded into bankruptcy court today to seek relief from its creditors.'' Rather used a similar writing strategy in his lead into a story about the conclusion of the trial of a former boxing champion: ''The rape trial of Mike Tyson is in its final round.''

The strategy is to use the words effectively, without becoming too cute or too distracting.

When Terry Anderson, the last American hostage in Lebanon, was released, Sam Donaldson led ABC's World News Tonight with this summary lead: ''America's long hostage crisis in the Middle East came to an end today.'' Taking a more personal approach, Dan Rather set a different tone for the story on the CBS evening news: ''Terry Anderson is on his way back home.'' Note how Donaldson's lead set a more detached tone and Rather's a more personal tone for a story that was clearly both historic and personal. An Associated Press reporter, Harry Rosenthal, accurately captured the spirit of another historic event when U.S. astronauts Neil Armstrong and Buzz Aldrin landed on the moon in 1969. There was a long delay while the two remained in the lunar module, putting on their special space suits. Rosenthal wrote: ''They kept the whole world waiting while they dressed to go out.''

The decline of communism in 1991 was captured effectively and unequivocally by Paul Duke, who led the PBS program ''Washington Week in Review'' with: ''The once powerful Soviet empire is now history.''

It doesn't take many words to write an effective lead if you understand the story and are able to cut right to its heart. In just eight words Duke captured the essence of one of the century's major stories.

These examples demonstrate skill in condensation. The best leads are simple. And clear. The language is conversational. They capture the substance and the tone of the story.

Advice from the Red Queen

The great editor Herbert Bayard Swope said the best rule for telling a story was laid down by the Red Queen in *Alice in Wonderland*. When asked how to tell a story, she explained, "Begin at the beginning, go through to the end and then stop." Some complicated stories have to be told this way, step by step, or the listener is lost.

Successful broadcast newswriters often talk their leads—and their stories—into their terminals. They may begin by asking themselves, "What's the lead?" More likely, the question is phrased, "Hey! You know what happened?" Then the lead comes more naturally, the story is phrased as if it were being told to a friend over lunch. What makes broadcast writing more difficult than luncheon conversation is the continual need for accuracy, brevity, and clarity—the ABCs. But the language you choose is roughly the same.

Finally, *listen* to the leads you hear on the air. Listen to how "story starting" is done by the pros. The real world of broadcast news should be the biggest, best classroom of all. And it's as close as your radio.

10. *The Lead-in*

Think of the lead-in as a tee setting up your video or audio report. It provides information for the listener's understanding of what follows. Normally it tells where the event occurred and when. In other words, it sets the scene. It identifies the reporter or speaker unless they identify themselves or a superimposed visual, called a "super," does the job. And it should be written in such a way that, without oversimplification or exaggeration, it generates interest. The lead-in should take no more time than necessary to meet these requirements. This is the *last* place in a story to be wordy.

Here is a typical lead-in:

> A decision by the United States Supreme Court makes it clear that the Court has become more conservative on civil rights issues. Carl Stern reports.

Observe that the lead-in consists of two basic parts. The first tells what the subject is and suggests what has happened. If it did more than suggest—in this instance, tell what the court said—there would be no need for the report. The second part introduces the reporter. Here the writer was succinct. Other lead-ins may have to be longer to "fill in" the listeners so they can understand, and appreciate, what they are about to see and hear. This lead-in, by Alex Chadwick of National Public Radio, provided necessary background for a live interview:

> Eighty years ago, the Norwegian explorer Raould Amundsen pitched a tent made of leather and silk, hoisted up the Norwegian flag, and marked the spot at which he became the first person to reach the South Pole.

The tent and the flag were seen four weeks later by the English explorer Robert Falcon Scott, who had been racing against Amundsen's team to reach the pole. He became the second person to set foot on the South Pole, and the last to see Raould Amundsen's flag.

Now a group of scientists from Norway, Sweden, Denmark, and Great Britain are heading back to the South Pole to try to find Amundsen's tent. On the line from Oslo to discuss this expedition is Dr. Olaph Orheim of the Norse Polar Institute.

The interview continued for about five minutes, describing the planned exploration. Listeners could understand the interviewee's explanations and descriptions because of the background and perspective provided by the lead-in.

There was no redundancy in Chadwick's lead-in and the interview, and there shouldn't be. Such duplication is scorned by broadcast journalists who sometimes call it "parroting" or the "round-robin effect." Former CBS News executive Emerson Stone refers to it as the "echo-chamber effect." On the air it sounds like this:

ANCHOR: The governor has called a special session of the legislature for July first. Here is Jeff Roberts.

ROBERTS: The governor has called a special session of the legislature. . . .

This sounds amateurish. It's also clumsy and wastes valuable time. The writer can usually introduce the report in an original way, using different words. And different facts. If this is difficult to do (and sometimes it is), one way to avoid the awkward redundancy is to cut the lead sentence from the tape and incorporate that information into your lead-in. Then pick up on the reporter's second sentence:

[A nuclear submarine has run aground in one of the main channels of Charleston harbor.] The Navy and Coast Guard ordered the harbor closed to all sea-going traffic until further notice. The sub has been identified by the Navy as the . .

In this case, the bracketed sentence was rephrased in the lead-in to make it "In the harbor of Charleston, South Carolina" and to include the name of the reporter. But it was worth the saving in air time.

Many stations and networks expect their reporters to provide a suggested lead-in for the newscast writers to work with. This practice makes sense because the reporter who covered the story usually has a good understanding of how the lead-in should relate to the reporter's audio or video package.

This lead-in from ABC's "World News Tonight" shows how closely the writer must work with the correspondent so the anchor's lead-in and reporter's package work effectively together. The lead-in was done by Sam Donaldson.

The United Nations today released a disturbing report on Iraq's refusal to come clean about its dangerous weapons programs. A special U-N commission says Baghdad's attitude toward cease-fire inspections continues to be one of obstruction and non-cooperation, particularly, says the commission, when it comes to potential nuclear capability. This new finding ensures that U-N-sponsored sanctions will remain in force, and it gives new urgency to the question of how long Iraq will be allowed to drag its feet. More on Iraq's obstructionism from ABC's John McWethy.

This led naturally into McWethy's package, which began:

Though much of the nuclear hardware was destroyed during the war, the Iraqi brain trust that built the program, largely from scratch, was not. . . .

It is easy to see that the writer had to know the background to the story, the substance of the story, and how the reporter began his package. When you add the obvious time requirements to a lead-in and package as detailed as this one, you can understand how well the various components must mesh for the story to have the clarity required.

In the early days of radio journalism it was common to say, "For that story, we switch to Paris, David Schoenbrun reporting." Or, "We take you now to City Hall, Charles Shaw reporting." You may occasionally still hear such introductions, but they are hackneyed and out of style. Anchors don't "switch" and "take you" as often as they used to—that's left to the engineers. Those phrases are now reserved for the times when television and radio do switch to a live report at the scene of an important story. Often it's simply "Rita Braver reports" or "Sam Donaldson has the story" or "John Cochran tells why."

It is good to vary your introductions. You will notice that we said "normally" the lead-in tells where and when something happened. Sometimes the lead-in *purposely* does not tell this. And it can be very effective, especially in introducing a feature story. Here's an example:

It's been the ranking sport in Europe and South America for years. It's the fastest-growing sport in the United States right now. The stars are internationally famous, and it's big business. What sport? James Walker fills you in. [Walker then talks about the popularity of soccer in the United States.]

This lead-in creates interest in the story. In such a lead-in, try to be creative. You can do it using only a few words. Like this:

In Texas, they're teaching policemen how to drive. Here is George Lewis.

You may not call that creative—it's so simple. That's part of the beauty of it. In six words you get an image that arouses curiosity, perhaps brings a smile.

Creativity. Something extra. An appreciation of the story. Another example of this was the lead-in used in 1974 by Walter Cronkite when the House Judiciary Committee began its hearing to determine whether, in its opinion, President Nixon should be impeached. Cronkite could have said

> In a few minutes, the House Judiciary Committee will start hearing testimony on a series of articles calling for the impeachment of the President.

Instead, he began his lead-in by saying

> Not in a hundred years has there been a day like today.

As he spoke, you saw the hearing room crowded with reporters and photographers as members of the committee came in and took their seats. The drama was about to begin, and Cronkite, by putting what was happening into historical perspective, had struck a dramatic note. The listener—the viewer in this instance—was tuned in.

You can write a lead-in without a verb, just as you can write leads without verbs. For example:

> After war—pestilence. Here is Richard Wagner in Saigon.

A lot depends on how a lead-in like this is read. It cannot be read rapidly. It must be read in a solemn, almost pedestrian way, with a pause after the word *war*. And each syllable of the phrase *after war* must be carefully articulated.

How about this lead-in?

> This is the kind of story that should start "Once upon a time." The story is told by Dick Schaap. [Schaap then told the Cinderella story of an awkward, ugly horse named Seattle Slew.]

Here again is a lead-in written in language that is marvelously simple. And notice how the anchor let Schaap tell the story. Too many anchors skim the cream off the story and then go to the correspondent for what's left. Here's an example of that kind of lead-in, which is a mistake.

> For the last eight weeks many thousand coal miners in Virginia, eastern Kentucky and Ohio have been out on a strike not authorized by their union, the United Mine Workers. This week-end the head of the U-M-W went on television to ask them to go back to work, but they're still out. And despite the lengthy wildcat strike, there's no shortage of coal. Bob Kur has more on the story.

Does he? It turns out he did, but so much information has been given in the lead-in that the listener's curiosity about the walkout has been satisfied.

Simplicity. And imagination.

Years ago, when he was a senior writer at CBS, Mervin Block composed—crafted—the most delightful lead-in we have ever seen. He wrote it for "The Sunday Night News." The anchor was Charles Osgood. Block lent us his carbon copy.

```
MB              OSGOOD  The New York City
                        marathon was won
                        today by an Italian.
                        He ran the 26
                        miles in two hours,
                        14 minutes,
                        53 seconds.
                        He got a good run for
                        his money and
                        good money for his
                        run.
                        Steve Young has the
                        story:
              VTR  TRACK UP
```

Just right. In four short sentences a lead-in that is four-star.

This story ran on the "CBS Evening News" on a night when Mike Wallace substituted for Dan Rather. The correspondent was Rita Braver. The story demonstrates how well a lead-in and a correspondent's lead can engage each other. It also demonstrates everything else we have been discussing: creativity, simplicity, and conversational style. Notice how readable Braver's sentences are and how easy it must have been for viewers to understand what she was saying. This is partly because most of her longer sentences are compound sentences. One of the secrets in broadcast newswriting is that, in terms of comprehension, one compound sentence equals two short sentences. Finally, as you read this script, observe how skillfully the words of the artist and those of the correspondent are integrated.

WALLACE: The Central Intelligence Agency is in the business of finding out other people's secrets, but the agency now has a pretty big secret of its own. Rita Braver tells the tale.

BRAVER: For months now, the secret has haunted this house of secrets.

JIM SANBORN (artist): Since the CIA commissioned it, I had to do something which was very distinctly "them."

BRAVER: So artist Jim Sanborn made Kryptos, a $250,000 sculpture that is also a giant encrypted puzzle, now standing in the very center of the CIA, stumping the agency's top spooks, spies, and cipherers.

SANBORN: There are several parts which are layered more deeply, so to speak, in—in encoding jargon. There are some very intently buried codes in here, which are—will be very, very difficult to crack.

BRAVER: Desperate CIA agents have resorted to asking for help from archrivals at other intelligence agencies, and Sanborn believes the race to solve the mystery began even as he was constructing Kryptos.

SANBORN: People were caught on ladders outside my building, trying to photograph through the windows, and some curious-looking individuals tried to get in the back of the building but were run off by the police.

BRAVER: Sanborn got a former CIA cryptographer, whose identity is also a secret, to help him create a message complex enough to confuse people whose very business is subterfuge.

SANBORN: I did that in a very calculating way. I did that in a very secretive way. And I'm hoping it will have that effect. I mean, somebody will figure it out, and then somebody'll forget what it said, and then they'll have to figure it out again, and so that's fine.

BRAVER: Sanborn has leaked a few clues. The message is linked to the CIA's own mission of communications and secrecy, and there's special significance in this section, the only one where the letters are unevenly spaced. He's revealed the message to only one man, CIA Director William Webster. Do you trust him to keep your secret?

SANBORN: I think I do. He winked at me when I gave it to him, and so . . .

BRAVER: As for predicting when all those superspooks will finally figure it out, the agency is typically non-committal.

PETER EARNEST (CIA officer): Whether this code will be cracked and this secret will be learned, only time will tell.

BRAVER: I want to give you a chance on ''CBS News'' to reveal the secret. Would you like this to be the place where you do it?

SANBORN: Now I can't do it more than ever, I suppose, because it's . . . the short sentences. Finally, as you read this script, observe how skillfully the words of the artist and those of the correspondent are integrated.

WALLACE: The Central Intelligence Agency is in the business of finding out other people's secrets, but the agency now has a pretty big secret of its own. Rita Braver tells the tale.

BRAVER: For months now, the secret has haunted this house of secrets.

JIM SANBORN (artist): Since the CIA commissioned it, I had to do something which was very distinctly "them."

BRAVER: So artist Jim Sanborn made Kryptos, a $250,000 sculpture that is also a giant encrypted puzzle, now standing in the very center of the CIA, stumping the agency's top spooks, spies, and cipherers.

SANBORN: There are several parts which are layered more deeply, so to speak, in—in encoding jargon. There are some very intently buried codes in here, which are—will be very, very difficult to crack.

BRAVER: Desperate CIA agents have resorted to asking for help from archrivals at other intelligence agencies, and Sanborn believes the race to solve the mystery began even as he was constructing Kryptos.

SANBORN: People were caught on ladders outside my building, trying to photograph through the windows, and some curious-looking individuals tried to get in the back of the building but were run off by the police.

BRAVER: Sanborn got a former CIA cryptographer, whose identity is also a secret, to help him create a message complex enough to confuse people whose very business is subterfuge.

SANBORN: I did that in a very calculating way. I did that in a very secretive way. And I'm hoping it will have that effect. I mean, somebody will figure it out, and then somebody'll forget what it said, and then they'll have to figure it out again, and so that's fine.

BRAVER: Sanborn has leaked a few clues. The message is linked to the CIA's own mission of communications and secrecy, and there's special significance in this section, the only one where the letters are unevenly spaced. He's revealed the message to only one man, CIA Director William Webster. Do you trust him to keep your secret?

SANBORN: I think I do. He winked at me when I gave it to him, and so . . .

BRAVER: As for predicting when all those superspooks will finally figure it out, the agency is typically non-committal.

PETER EARNEST (CIA officer): Whether this code will be cracked and this secret will be learned, only time will tell.

BRAVER: I want to give you a chance on "CBS News" to reveal the secret. Would you like this to be the place where you do it?

SANBORN: Now I can't do it more than ever, I suppose, because it's . . . the more . . . the more interested everybody becomes, the more interested I am in keeping the secret.

BRAVER: Now where have we heard that before? Rita Braver, "CBS News," at the CIA.

WALLACE: And that is the "CBS Evening News." Bob Schieffer will be here tomorrow; Susan Spencer, on Sunday, just before "60 Minutes." I'm Mike Wallace in New York. Good night.

(ANNOUNCEMENTS)

Although this report consists of talking heads, it is dominated by video, footage showing an extraordinary sculpture commissioned by the CIA. Nowhere does Braver describe the sculpture. That would be redundant; the viewer, seeing it, needs no description. Note how Wallace's lead-in creates interest and how Braver has written her lead so that it connects to the lead-in, making a smooth transition. The suggestion of a haunted house is a nice touch. This is an ideal lead. It's beautifully simple and effective.

Perhaps you caught the quarter-million-dollar cost of the sculpture written "$250,000," instead of "250-thousand dollars." This is a transcript. The typist wasn't writing broadcast style.

A writer must take special care when reports begin with natural sound rather than the correspondent's voice. It is important that the natural sound be identified for the listener immediately. Sometimes that identification can be general, but there are stories in which the description must be exact. Such was the case April 28, 1969 at CBS Radio News as Richard C. Hottelet introduced a taped report from Paris about the resignation of President Charles de Gaulle. The tape began with ten seconds of natural sound, and then the sound continued under the voice of correspondent Peter Kalischer. Hottelet's introduction read:

> Thousands of Frenchmen gathered in the streets and sang, "Adieu, De Gaulle." Peter Kalischer stood and listened.

Those in the radio audience also listened and understood what they heard—even the singing. Hottelet had adroitly tuned their ears to receive those words set to music. He knew that phrases sung or chanted by a crowd frequently are less distinct than the same words spoken directly into the microphone. Listeners weren't distracted by uncertainty over the actuality and were able to appreciate Kalischer's report. It explained how the singing of "Adieu, De Gaulle" symbolized the mood of the French people, beset by economic and social turmoil.

De Gaulle seemed to want a vote of confidence when he called a national referendum on a minor proposal that didn't have to be submitted to the people. He threatened to resign if voters rejected it. They did, and De Gaulle quit the same day, causing Kalischer to report:

The issue was important to no one but De Gaulle. He's like a man who could stride across mountains but stumbled on a pebble. . . . It's as if someone able to walk on water drowned in a puddle.

This graphic and thought-provoking assessment made its mark in the listener's mind. And a good lead-in had helped guide it there, by answering in advance any questions that might have derailed the listener's train of thought.

Many radio stations and some radio networks have developed their own shorthand style for newscasts running no more than one or two minutes. If you are writing for such a program, the limited time forces you to be less complete. You can't provide much background. In your lead-in, you might not introduce the correspondent by name.

These minicasts require special care. As more facts are omitted, it becomes easier to distort. And this word of caution: if your station's style calls for *not* identifying the reporter in the lead-in, the first voice on the tape should be that of the reporter, not that of an unidentified newsmaker.

In this chapter we have described a variety of standard, conventional policies and practices for writing lead-ins. If you violate one of them, you should understand that you are violating it. And you should know why—for what purpose—you are violating it (perhaps for dramatic effect, or because it conflicts with your station's style).

Lead-outs

Whether you call them lead-outs or tag lines or caps, they mean the same thing. They are what comes immediately after the audio or video tape and, with the lead-in, complete the wrap-around. The lead-out is a stylistic luxury in television but often a necessity in radio. Its basic function is to reidentify the person heard in an actuality so as to remove any doubt. Television, of course, has visuals to do this job.

It's not uncommon to hear a string of actualities in a newscast with lead-outs no more varied than, "That was Governor Cuomo," "That was Senator Kennedy," or "That was Mayor Daley." This is stilted writing. It usually identifies a lazy writer. Ideally, the lead-out does more than reidentify. It adds something to the story or provides a bridge to the next item, or both.

The best writers intentionally reserve at least one fact from the story to include at the conclusion of the tape, a tactic that gives them an opportunity to reintroduce unobtrusively the name of the speaker who has just been heard. For example, at the conclusion of a taped report on Senator John Chafee's bill to ban the manufacture and sale of handguns, the lead-out might read "Senator Chafee says violators could be imprisoned for up to five years and fined up to five thousand dollars." Note that this lead-out begins with the name of the newsmaker who appears on the tape and briefly and clearly adds one more piece of information to the story.

11. *The Spoken Word*

H. V. Kaltenborn used to say, "St. Paul said it 1900 years ago, 'Except ye utter by the tongue words easy to be understood, how shall it be known what is spoken? For ye shall speak into the air.'"

It is humbling to realize that a preacher almost twenty centuries ago not only predicted the advent of radio but also said just about the most important thing there is to say about writing news for broadcast, which is that the broadcaster, no matter how complex the subject, must report that complexity "uttering by the tongue words easy to be understood."

But the fleetingness of your news—this speaking into the air—requires more. It demands that words, properly chosen, be properly read. While good reading enhances a good script, many a good script has been butchered by bad reading.

Here are some reading tips.

• Understand the story. That is the first requirement. It's hard to sound intelligent about something you don't comprehend. (You may get away with it for a while, but one day you will trip yourself up.)

• Appreciate what you are saying. Do not read the story of the death of a child in the street the same way you would read an election return. You are not a robot. So recognize the difference.

• Read at a natural pace. The only excuse for hurrying through a story is if you are running out of time. Too often well-written stories are ruined by anchors who seem to want to get through them as quickly as possible. Well-written stories deserve to be read well. Anyone who races through the news is saying it is not interesting or important. Haste also reduces comprehension. The words come so fast listeners miss the story. Remember, this is news on the air. The listener has to understand the first, and only, time around.

• Rehearse. Not only will you be less apt to stumble, but you will see where to mark your copy for pauses and the words you want to stress. Reading aloud also can help you discover troublesome tongue-twisters.

• Know the value of the pause. Certainly the advertisers know. In the corn flakes commercial we're told, "Try them again [pause] for the first time." In the electric razor commercial, it's "We made close [pause] comfortable." And, for heaven's sake, brake for periods. Don't be one of those people who, trying to sound different, bash their audiences by running sentences together. Also, you owe it to your listeners to pause between stories.

Murrow was endowed with a rich baritone voice. His reading skill was renowned. Yet for best performance he felt duty-bound to mark his script for pauses. His pause marks frequently were exaggerated commas, such as you see in the original copy below. (And, incidentally, note the simple, direct language.) This is the lead for his radio broadcast of February 6, 1952.

This is the News —

```
    The British have a new Queen.   King George the Sixth died in his sleep

last night at the age of 56.   His daughter, Queen Elizabeth, is due in

London tomorrow, (flying back from Kenya.)   Here is a recorded report from

Howard K. Smith in London, telling us how Her Majesty's subjects reacted

to the news.


    TAPE:
```

Murrow indicated longer pauses with a slash, like this /. He also underscored words for emphasis.

David Brinkley may have broadcasting's most distinctive way of reading, which is also his distinctive way of speaking. Here is a sentence with his markings. If you read it aloud, stressing the words he underlined, you will find yourself doing a fair imitation of Brinkley.

```
One requirement for success in running a government or private

operation is staffing the place with competent and reliable people.
```

Don Hewitt, executive producer of "60 Minutes," says, "I'm a bug on writing and delivery. I will frequently tell a correspondent that a pause is too long, or not long enough, or that an inflection is wrong. Is that dramatic coaching? No, that's editing. Inflections and pauses are to us what commas and semi-colons are to print people."

Hewitt, the most successful producer in broadcast news, recognizes that inflection and judicious use of the pause are vital elements in the editorial process.

• In speaking on the air, beware of sibilants.

When Jodie Foster won an Oscar for her performance in "Silence of the Lambs," a critic said on television: "She had these dreams of some-day savoring success." Because of all those sibilants—all those *s*'s—the critic seemed to hiss.

In what you write, in what you ad lib, avoid a succession of ess sounds that make for slush. Don't (unless trying to prove something) attempt a sentence like "Sheriff Stickney said someone smuggled the saw into Smith's cell." For many a broadcaster such a sentence has brought disaster.

Some sentences can be helped by killing the *s* attached to a noun. In each of the following sentences the *s* in parenthesis is surplus.

"They saw no sign(s) the Iraqis would back down."
"He was stung by their criticism(s)."
"It gave him no advantage(s)."
"She entertained no thought(s) of resigning."
"He spoke of their hope(s) for social reform."

With the elimination of the *s,* each sentence not only sounds better but is easier to read.

In one of his columns, George Will wrote, "It is with nouns denoting substance that socialists nowadays are abstemious." It is a sentence, slippery with *s*'s, that Will, a master craftsman with words, might not have written for broadcast. (Nor, we hope, would he employ *abstemious,* an adjective that means "marked by restraint." On second thought, he just might. He is one of those scholar-journalists like Bill Buckley who enjoy using words whose meanings you can only suspect.)

In the same column, Will speaks of Neil Kinnock, leader of the British Labor Party, as being "more prolix [there he goes again] than Hubert Humphrey was, but without Humphrey's honest passions or serious purposes." The sentence and its meaning would have been stronger if Will had omitted the *s* from the nouns *passions* and *purposes. Passion* and *purpose* have more impact. Purpose is a big thing. So is passion. The world is full of small passions and petty purposes.

• Read with expression. (Perhaps, back in grade school, you had a teacher who told you that.) The words you use have different worth and warrant different treatment. This is a matter of emphasizing those words that contribute most. Ann Utterback, the speech expert, says, "Find the meaning-laden words. If copy is well written, there will generally be one meaning-laden word in each phrase." She says these words should be underlined.

Bart Giamatti was commissioner of baseball. He was also a poet and president of Yale. He said of baseball, "It breaks your heart. It is designed to break your heart." A good reader will underline—stress—the verb *designed.* The emphasis helps. It intensifies meaning.

Sometimes the emphasis is misplaced, as in the case of the anchor who, stressing the last word, said, "They recognized it was an annual *problem.*" The stress, of course, should have been on *annual.* "They recognized it was an *annual* problem." The fact that this is a recurring problem is made more apparent. Some newscasters think that bearing down on sentence endings gives them a distinctive style. Indeed, it does set them apart—as amateurish.

• Listen to the cadences, to the rhythms in what you write—the sound. Do your sentences, when you read them aloud, seem to clump along or do they flow gracefully? We think of the last lines in Eric Sevareid's commentary upon the assassination of Martin Luther King: "So the label on his life must not be 'a long day's journey into night.' It must be 'a long night's journey into day.' "

• With extraordinary footage, you can heighten the effect by saying nothing. Two examples:

On April 8, 1974, Hank Aaron hit his 715th home run and broke Babe Ruth's record. The crowd and the television announcer went crazy with excitement. Then came the replay, and the announcer, calmer now, said, "Here it is again. You can watch. I'll just shut up." Millions of viewers relived the moment: the batter coiling for the swing, the hard crack of the ball on the bat, and the man, rhythmic, rounding the bases. Thanks to the announcer's good sense, the thing that had happened seemed enshrined.

On September 2, 1990, at the height of the Gulf crisis, an Iraqi 747 brought home the first American refugees from Baghdad. "NBC Nightly News" showed, in silence, the airliner landing at Andrews Air Force Base outside Washington. The picture was much, much stronger because no one spoke.

There is a time to be still.

12. *Voice-over: Image and the Word*

Whether you write news for radio or television, the style is much the same. The writing must be concise and so highly readable as to be conversational. Facts must be selected so that the story will be truthfully represented. And these facts—these words—must be arranged in such a way that the meaning is clear. The listener (and the television viewer is also a listener) must understand what you are saying, or the whole complicated, expensive, important electronic news process is for naught.

So radio news and television news have this basic common denominator—style. However, television journalism often requires the writer to perform a function alien to radio reporting and writing. We refer, of course, to the matching of word with picture—writing scripts to be read over videotape, maps, charts, and other graphics. This is writing the voice-over (VO). In it, words and pictures should clearly complement each other.

Beginners tend to overwrite VO. They state the obvious, telling the viewers what they can see for themselves, thus creating redundancies. Or they pack too many words into the script. This makes readers of voice-over copy race to keep up with the tape. And by racing they often make mistakes. The object is a voice-over script that can be read at a natural pace, a script with fewer words than the maximum that can be read in the allotted time.

Seasoned practitioners of television news know when to shut up and let the picture carry the story. "Writing a silence," says John Hart, "is as important as writing words. We don't rely on video enough." Be sensitive to the interplay between word and picture. Produce narration that not only reinforces or explains but also contains pauses for those places where the picture needs no words—pauses of three seconds, five seconds, ten seconds, or more.

Writing news for television is communicating to the viewers what they don't see or understand. "We are a verbal society," said pioneer producer Fred Friendly. "We're also a picture society. People are much more experienced at seeing things on film than they ever were before. They seek out elements. They fasten onto little facts out there. They may know more from looking at that picture than the reporter knows, especially if they're brighter, more perceptive. So for the writer just to recite the obvious is what our young people call 'Dullsville.' " Friendly noted that writers have to understand more about their subjects: they've got to tell the viewers something they don't already know.

Former NBC News President Reuven Frank said, "Pictures are different from words. They are not illustrations of words. They are a different dimension of information. Pictures are as different from words as smells are from sounds, but all four of those are kinds of information." Frank believes words convey mainly information, whereas pictures carry more emotion. As he puts is, "What are the best pictures from an airplane crash? A silk stocking hanging from a tree, a doll with a broken face, waiting relatives. These, in their own way, can tell you more than someone saying in words how many died. . . . Even when such pictures are used, some voice is talking about something else."

If this sounds elementary, it is. If it sounds like needless advice, it is not, as a viewer can see by watching almost any action story in a newscast.

Some visual stories need virtually no narration. Compelling video of a celebration, a military battle, a dramatic rescue, or a close race may not need any explanatory script, except for some background. Overscripting in such cases can distract.

On the Road

Charles Kuralt of CBS has developed a deserved reputation for the quality of writing in his stories, many of which appeared as "On the Road" reports. Most of these stories were small masterpieces, notable for their cinematography and voice-over narration, written by Kuralt. In a style reminiscent of John Steinbeck's *Travels with Charley,* Kuralt and his crew roamed the country in a camper. They visited such out-of-the-way places as Castine, Maine; Red Lodge, Montana; Jackrabbit, Arizona; and Deep Gap, North Carolina. They reported from a small white-steepled community in Vermont simply because the community was lovely and they wanted to shoot a low-key story on the delights of autumn. Kuralt always was personally involved in the shooting, peering through the lens and taking notes, so he could build the story as they shot it. He said, "I seem to write the pieces in my head. By the time I start typing, they're pretty much done."

The artful blending of image and word is clear in this Kuralt report on the demise of the famous train, the Cannonball Express:

CRONKITE (ON CAMERA):

Charles Kuralt, who's been on the road reporting Americana for this program, rode the rails on his latest assignment, and that's not easy in this day of disappearing passenger trains--even those once famed in story and song.

BARROOM SCENE: BOB WALLER SINGING
''WABASH CANNONBALL'' TO BANJO AC-
COMPANIMENT. SONG CONTINUES OVER AER-
IAL SHOTS OF TRAIN PASSING THROUGH
COUNTRYSIDE.

KURALT (ON CAMERA):

In a bar near Blooming-ton, Indiana, Bob Waller and Wayne Schuman are asked to do the song almost every night. The Wabash Cannon-ball is as much a part of Indiana as the small towns and the rivers and the cornfields.

CUT TO CLOSE-UP OF TRAIN

''Listen to the jingle and the rumble and the roar.''

CUT TO INTERIOR OF DINING CAR

You can still ride the Wabash Cannonball, but you'd better hurry. It's all going, all this--the gleaming white tablecloth with the single red carna-tion facing you, the sound of the great train rushing through the morning from St. Louis to Detroit. The day of the passenger train is nearly over, and this sound is nearly an echo now.

RECEDING SOUND OF TRAIN'S WHISTLE

INTERCUT OF EXTERIOR AND INTERIOR OF
TRAIN TO MATCH NARRATION

The Norfolk and Western Railroad is asking the In-terstate Commerce Commis-sion to permit this train to be discontinued. A year from now, the Wabash Cannonball will very likely have passed into history. The first Cannonball went roaring down the tracks in 1884, the yellow light of its oil lamps in its elegant smokers and parlor coaches flashing through the cornfields. But that's all over now. The people go by car and stay at Howard Johnson motor lodges, and the Cannonball's seats are empty. It has shrunk to a pitiful short train, passing the silos of Illinois, whistling mournfully for the country crossroads of Indiana almost by force of habit now.

INTERCUTS (CONT'D.)

This is a part of America we knew as children, and our children will never really know. They will

CLOSE-UP OF COUPLINGS

never hear the jingle of the couplings, the squeal of the wheels on the curves. They will never hear the conductor's song.

CONDUCTOR SEEN AND HEARD CALLING OUT
NEXT STOP

Wabash is the next station stop. Wabash. This way out!

FOOTAGE OF TRAIN PASSING THROUGH

The Cannonball still stops at Wabash, also at Granite City, Mount Olive, Stonington, Decatur, Lafayette. Night overtakes the train at Delphi, and it goes on to Peru, Fort Wayne, Montpelier, but hardly anybody ever gets on or off. Once this was the way young men left Wabash or Milan or Edwardsville to seek their fortunes in the big cities. Those are old

CUT TO CLEMENT SILENT	men now and Norfolk and Western Vice President Walter Clement says not enough of them ride the Cannonball to make the train pay its way.
CLEMENT:	You won't believe this. The latest figures show 24 people a day in the entire state of Indiana have used the Wabash Cannonball. Twenty-four a day.
AERIALS OF TRAIN	So this train, like so many others, is about to die. Set your watch by the Cannonball while you may. Pause at the crossroads to let her pass. Take one last look. Tomorrow, the Wabash Cannonball won't be a train at all, only a banjo tune.
CUT TO WALLER SINGING MORE OF ``WABASH CANNONBALL'' BALLAD CUT TO KURALT RIDING ON TRAIN KURALT:	Charles Kuralt, CBS News, aboard the Wabash Cannonball.

In telling this story, Kuralt had a wonderful time with the names of towns. He played on them, almost like musical notes. He milked the nostalgia in the story, which he recognized as its strongest element. He made expert use of alliteration, which is to say he used the device without beating the listener over the head with it. Consider, for example, the successive use of *l*'s in "yellow light of the oil lamps in its elegant smokers and parlor coaches flashing through the cornfields." He may not have done it consciously, but the effect is there, working for him. His craftsmanship also shows in his selection of specific detail—the flower on the table is a "single red carnation," the light is "yellow," the farms are "fields of corn," the motorists stay at "Howard Johnson motor lodges." The train doesn't just pass through Illinois, it passes "the silos of Illinois." It is "the couplings" of the train that jingle. The young ambitious men boarded the express at specific places: Wabash, Milan, Edwardsville. And certainly a factor in the good writing is that Kuralt felt the story. It clearly meant something to him.

The idea of doing video features like "On the Road" has spread to several stations around the country. Instead of rambling through the whole United States, these reporters and their crews crisscross their individual states or regions. About once a week, WISC-TV in Madison, Wisconsin, airs a popular news feature called "News 3 Traveler," with Mark Koehn.

The following is an example of one of Koehn's scripts, including the cues, as he uses them, for video and for sound on tape (*SOT*):

ANCHOR LEAD-IN	We hear a lot of talk these days about the decline of our small rural communities. Talk of business districts shriveling up. Well, take a trip to the small village of Keyeser, which straddles the Dane and Columbia County line. News 3 Traveler Mark Koehn did, and what he found may surprise you.
SOT--KOEHN STAND-UP DOWNTOWN STREET & STORES	This is the village of Keyeser, a crossroads if ever there's been one. You can stand smack-dab in the middle of Keyeser and get a sunburn before you'd have to get out of the way of a car. Quiet, Keyeser is. At least on the surface. But there's something of a battle brewing here.
EXTERIORS--2 STORES	On one side, there's Glenn Gullickson's. On the other it's Ester Gilbertson's.
INTERCUT SHOTS--2 STORES	Glenn Gullickson and Ester Gilbertson. What we have here in tiny Keyeser, population, oh, about 40 or so, are *two* general stores. Glenn Gullickson's place to the west, Ester Gilbertson's to the east. The two stores stare at each other in the summer heat. Gullickson's and Gilbertson's. It's been this way in Keyeser since 1894. For almost a hundred years these two stores have been competing.
SOT--ESTER & GLENN	[We're both happy to be here - have always been competing - That's the way we were brought up.]
PRODUCTS INSIDE STORES	These days Ester's is a little busier than Glenn's. While Glenn has one can of chocolate syrup, Ester has over a dozen. Ester carries flannel shirts and overalls and shoes, while Glenn . . .

SOT--GLENN	[We used to sell a lot of shoes, but sold the last pair about two years ago. We once had five, six hundred pairs of shoes at one time.]
SOT--ESTER	[Business has been pretty good. I can't complain. I'll keep doing this as long as my legs hold out.]
CUSTOMERS AT ESTER'S BAR	Ester also has a beer bar in the back of the store, and that really brings in the customers. But mostly folks stop for soda or cigarettes. We can call the competition friendly. Oh, Ester does offer free water, and Glenn caters to the sports crowd. But there's no price gouging or that sort of thing. And that's understandable. Glenn and Ester are first cousins.
SOT--CUSTOMERS TALKING	[She's a fine lady. . . . He's one of the nicest people in town. . . .]
INTERCUTS--ESTER & GLENN	So if you need a soda, even a greeting card . . . or how about a 70-year-old box of cumin or a rusted-out can of radiator rust inhibitor . . . you know where to go. And the best thing is, you have your choice of two stores.
SOT--ESTER & GLENN	[No, we're not trying to run each other out of business.]
SOT--KOEHN STAND-UP	We're happy to report that in Keyeser, the country store is alive and well. Both of them. Traveling in Keyeser, I'm Mark Koehn, WISC News Three.

Note how Koehn captures the small-town informality in his script: "a crossroads if ever there's been one," and "here in tiny Keyeser, population, oh, 40 or so." He also makes excellent use of specific references: "one can of chocolate syrup" and "flannel shirts and overalls and shoes." Note especially how effectively the script and the video supplement each other. While we're seeing the exteriors of the two stores, the script fills in a detail we can't see, that "almost a hundred years these two stores have been competing." And while we're seeing customers in the stores, we hear "There's no price gouging or that sort of thing. And that's understandable. Glenn and Ester are first cousins."

In television, words and pictures are twins.

A horror story of the 1990s is the campaign of ethnic cleansing carried out by Serbian forces in Bosnia. Giselle Fernandez wrote and narrated this report for the CBS evening news.

VOICE-OVER: PREGNANT WOMAN PACING HOSPITAL CORRIDOR	In a Sarajevo hospital, this 30-year-old woman anxiously waits to rid her body of the baby growing inside her, the baby she associates with hate, not love.
VOICE-OVER: WOMEN WEEPING	She is one of an estimated 20-thousand Muslim women who claim Serbian soldiers, under direct orders, kidnaped, raped and wilfully impregnated them.
SOUND ON TAPE: TRANSLATOR	WOMAN SAYS SHE FEELS DIRTY, DOESN'T WANT TO SEE THE BABY. ''IF I SEE IT, I WILL STRANGLE IT.''
VOICE-OVER: NATURAL SOUND SHOOTING, PEOPLE RUNNING FOR COVER, BODIES, BURIALS	Reports of an alarming number of rapes is just the latest in a long list of atrocities emerging from that war-torn country: concentration camps, ethnic cleansing
VOICE-OVER: CHILDREN IN WOMEN'S ARMS, LYING IN BED	and now testimonials from women in refugee camps claiming they are victims of ethnic breeding, much like the Nazi program to create an Aryan nation.
SOUND ON TAPE: ANURA GNADA-DASON, WORLD COUNCIL OF CHURCHES	CITES TESTIMONY OF WOMEN WHO HAVE BEEN RAPED.
SOUND ON TAPE: CHRISTINA DOCTARE, WORLD HEALTH ORGANIZATION	DESCRIBES WHAT IS HAPPENING IN BOSNIA AS ETHNIC-CIDE.
VOICE-OVER: CONFESSED RAPIST WALKS TOWARD AND PAST CAMERA	In a Bosnian prison, this Serbian soldier confessed to raping and killing Muslim women in detention camps. He said he was following direct orders and even demonstrated his method of execution. He will be the first Serbian sol-

	dier tried in Bosnia for war crimes.
FERNANDEZ ON CAMERA	The United Nations and the European Community Council have strongly condemned what they call this act of unspeakable brutality. They are demanding that all the detention camps in former Yugoslavia be shut down, but especially the brothels where girls as young as seven and women as old as 60 are being detained, tortured and raped.
VOICE-OVER: VARIOUS SHOTS BODIES, GRAVES, PEOPLE GRIEVING	For many women and their babies it's already too late. There are reportedly thousands of unwanted children whose parents have been killed. Others from rape are yet to be born. What will become of them?

In this piece, pictures serve purely to illustrate the story. They do not themselves report, as did video of the explosion of the Challenger and the beating by Los Angeles police of Rodney King, to cite two extreme examples.

Fernandez does not tell viewers what they can see for themselves. In talking about the confessed rapist, she doesn't speak of his unsavory appearance. Viewers know. They're looking at him.

She uses lean, incisive language. She could have said something like "This 30-year-old woman is pregnant and abhors her condition." Instead, she chose "This 30-year-old woman *waits to rid her body of the baby growing inside her.*" Now we almost feel the woman's revulsion.

And Fernandez uses few adjectives. She knows the strength of a script lies in its nouns and verbs.

Sometimes the reporter should say less and let others—those involved in the story—say more. When a small church in Westmoreland County, Pennsylvania, burned to the ground, arson was suspected. There had been other suspicious fires in the area. In her report the next day, Mary Robb Jackson of KDKA-TV gave members of the church, and its pastor, room to express their feelings. She recognized that it was their words, not hers, that would "make" the story. She chose her own words well. Observe how, for emphasis in reading, she set apart the line "They had no insurance." Jackson says that in this piece she was blessed with excellent photography.

{WIDE SHOT:WITH AUDIO UNDER}	>>''Life can come out of these here dry ashes. These ashes are not

dead--they are still alive--oh yes.''

{TAPE 1/6:26:09}

>>THE TINY CONGREGATION OF THE NEW HOPE BAPTIST CHURCH STOOD IN THE MORNING CHILL AND CHARRED RUINS, PRAYING FOR THOSE WHO HAD TRES-PASSED AGAINST THEM.

{TAPE 1/ 7:02:21}

>>But, Father, the enemy is all over the land--let us that's sup-posed to be Christians have a hum-ble heart--and have mercy on these people.''

*CG 2L02
SCOTT HAVEN
Westmoreland Co.

>>THIS HAS BEEN HALLOWED GROUND FOR OVER A HUNDRED YEARS. THE BAP-TIST CHURCH TOOK OVER IN THE EARLY FIFTIES WHEN THE VILLAGE OF SCOTTHAVEN WAS A BUSTLING COAL TOWN.

''IT WAS THEN THAT THE REVEREND RITA JONES, WITH HER HUSBAND AS DEACON, BEGAN THEIR MINISTRY HERE. THEY HAVE SUSTAINED IT ON HIS PENSION AND SOCIAL SECURITY.

''THEY HAD NO INSURANCE.''

{TAPE 1/23:50:19}
*CG SB2
DEACON FRANK JONES
New Hope Baptist Church
{TAPE 2/15:39:25}
*CG sb2
REV. RITA JONES
New Hope Baptist Church

>>I worried more about this building than I do about my own home--because God must come first.

>>I wasn't ashamed to get used furniture off the street to bring it here to paint it to make the church over. I wasn't ashamed to get old carpets that people had put out so that my church could look pretty.''

*CG JACKSREP

>>BERNIE KASSLER AND HIS FATHER, LAWRENCE, WHO LIVE CLOSE TO THE CHURCH, TRIED TO KEEP AN EYE ON IT BECAUSE THERE HAVE BEEN A NUMBER OF FIRES IN THE AREA IN THE PAST FEW YEARS - TEENAGERS PARTY IN A NEARBY

STRIP MINE - AND THE CHURCH HAD
BEEN VANDALIZED BEFORE.''

{TAPE 1/19:53:05}
*CG SB2
LAWRENCE KASSLER
Neighbor

>>We talked about that. We talked
about that you know, said you know
before too long they're gonna burn
the old church down and by God they
did. It's a shame, it's a shame.

{TAPE 2/9:00:04}
*CG sb2
MARY FRANCES DRAKE
Church Member

>>This is a very sad day--very sad.
I am a child of God and I just don't
believe--I don't believe people
could do things like this.

>>So I just pray to God he give me
strength that one day we may be
able to raise this up again. We
can't do it by ourselves--we got
to have help.

{TAPE 1/ 21:39:07}

>>Why . . .Why . . .Why . . . ?

>>MARY ROBB JACKSON, KDKA-EYE-
WITNESS NEWS.''

Picture over Voice

Most narration is written to go with video that's already shot. But sometimes it's the other way around, and the script is written first. Such scripts are often carefully constructed essays that develop a thought by using a combination of non-photographable abstracts and concrete examples that can be portrayed visually.

A number of these essays were televised during the thirty-one hours of continuous coverage of man's first landing on the moon. They were needed to complement the central action and to fill those time periods when astronauts Aldrin, Armstrong, and Collins would either be out-of-touch or would have nothing to report. One of these essays, dealing with the moon and the earth's tides, was written for CBS by Jeff Gralnick and narrated by Charles Kuralt. Here is part of that script, which shows how pictures are used to cover words.

VARIOUS SHOTS OF SEACOAST.
TIDES MOVING IN AND OUT
:36

The seas have rolled for
millions of years, swirling
around the continents,
pulled in ebbs and flows, responsible to nothing except
the moon, a quarter million
miles away. Twice each day,
as the earth revolves, it

presents first one face, then the other, to the moon. And as it does, that heavenly-body so far away pulls and tugs at the seas of the earth, causing the waters to roll in dramatically, sweeping all before them in a majestic rush for shore, whipping up waves as the moon seemingly tries to drag the oceans from their floors.

QUIET EMPTY BEACHES
:15

And then the tide recedes as the moon moves away. The seas fall back, leaving bare the strands of glistening sands, which would have remained covered forever were it not for the inexorable pull of the moon riding silently out in space.

PEACEFUL BEACH
:05

The tide can drift in easily, kissing the shore, or it can be whipped in mightily in great, crashing, storm-driven waves that force people from the beaches.

PEOPLE STANDING ON BULKHEADS,
WATCHING THE SEA
:15

But never too far, because there seems nothing so majestic as the sea enraged, driven by the wind, pulled by the moon. So inexorable is the tide, so relentless, that across a span of several centuries--a drop in the bucket

SHOTS OF ABBEY OF
MONT ST MICHEL
:25

of time--the tide turned the French abbey Mont St. Michel from a tree-surrounded refuge near the coast to an island outpost, a fortress protected by high walls. And, once a day, by high tide. Tide that is tugged by the moon until it surrounds the old fort with waters more than 60 feet deep, covering the road that leads to it, protecting

	it completely in a way no knight of old could have hoped, or planned his castle to make it safe.
LS FORTRESS :03	Man couldn't protect this fortress as well as the moon.
DISSOLVE TO SEAGULL SUPERED OVER-FULL MOON :15	One myth-maker once likened the moon to a great silver bird circling above the earth, lighting the earth, brushing the sea with its wing-tips, piling up the oceans' waters as it flew overhead.
LOSE THE SEAGULL, SEE ONLY FULL MOON :10	Now two men sit on the moon, looking down at the blue earth, at the waters of earth, controlled so long by the moon and still answering only to it.

This piece was aired on July 20, 1969. The astronauts had reached the moon, but Armstrong still had not taken his first step. There would be a wait of more than three hours between the landing and the historic first walk, which explains use of the verb *sit*—"Now two men sit on the moon." Neither Armstrong nor Aldrin had yet emerged from the lunar module.

When Gralnick furnished this script, he remarked in an accompanying letter: "While it is a good illustration of words and pictures matching, it strikes me that it also shows how a writer in television, or radio, has as a prime responsibility the job of making words sound as though the man speaking had written them for himself. I think only Kuralt could have delivered that piece. Had I written it for anyone else, it would have been done differently."

A Final Important Point

We've saved a cardinal rule for this concluding paragraph: Don't let the words fight the picture. Make one match the other. Remember that narration should explain and identify what viewers can't see for themselves, while reinforcing and elaborating on what can be seen. Sometimes a counterpoint between image and words can be effective, with the right material and an expert writer. But most voice-over writing should relate to the picture. Conflicts between words and picture confuse the viewer, and can cause that particular endeavor in television journalism to fail in its primary goal of informing those who watch and listen.

13. *Those Special Formats*

Most broadcast journalists begin as generalists. At that first job in a small radio market they probably rise well before dawn to prepare and anchor early morning newscasts, visit local government offices for stories during the day, anchor late afternoon newscasts, and even cover night meetings of the city council or county board. In addition, they may occasionally do sportscasts, farm market reports, and weather forecasts. If that first job is in small market television, they may be reporter, photographer, editor, producer, and weekend anchor. They, too, may occasionally fill in doing sports, weather, and agricultural reports.

But as their careers move into larger markets, the jobs become less general, and specific career tracks unfold. They become newscast producers, anchors, videotape editors, sports reporters, assignment editors, meteorologists, or special projects producers. In this chapter we will discuss two of the more popular specializations in broadcast news—magazine reporting and sports reporting.

Although the networks still produce occasional documentaries, far more attention is now devoted to newsmagazine programs. This genre has been spawned to a great extent by the commercial and critical success of CBS's "60 Minutes." This hugely successful program (rated more than once as the most popular program on network television for an entire season) has paved the way for other networks, and many local stations, to develop magazine programs of their own. They vary in format, but most use the personnel and expertise of the news department or division to develop a type of extended, in-depth reporting that is not possible within the constraints of daily journalism. In addition, such programs appeal to network and station management because their production cost is generally far less than that of entertainment programing.

In some cases the staff for the magazine program is made up news reporters, producers, and anchors who are assigned exclusively to the magazine. At other stations, different news staffers contribute to different editions of the program.

Although the magazine program and the news program require the same basic functions to produce—reporting, writing, editing, producing, and anchoring—there is at least one significant difference between them: the magazine is free of many of the day-to-day constraints of the newscast, both in production time and story length. The stories can run longer and be more fully developed, and the reporter, writer, and producer can generally take the time required to do a more in-depth job.

For example, on many of the network and local magazine programs currently on television it is not unusual for the main stories on a program to run between eight and twelve minutes. To a reporter used to meeting a producer's demand to do a complicated story in a minute and fifteen seconds, this additional time seems a luxury. But stories on magazine programs are far more than extended news stories. The additional time allows not only more investigative reporting, but also more creative use of video and natural sound. They are usually not late-breaking stories that require inclusion of the latest angle.

For instruction (and not a little enjoyment) read the following story about how the New York Yankees acquired a pitcher named Brien Taylor. It was reported by Morley Safer for "60 Minutes" on February 16, 1992. The original script ran fifteen pages. We have shortened it slightly.

The scene is Beaufort, North Carolina, described by Safer as as "a coastal community separated by some waterways and by race."

SAFER: The white part is southern grace and
                         charm. Beaufort by the Sea, they call
                         it. The black part is called North
                         River, formerly Fishtown. A cluster of
                         small homes, shacks, trailers, and a
                         small but spirited church.

(CHURCH MUSIC)   Decades come and go without much chang-
SAFER: ing in places like Beaufort. But 25
                         years ago, Beaufort, like the rest of
                         America, changed dramatically. For the
                         first time, black children were al-
                         lowed to attend school with whites. But
                         so wrenching was that event here at East
                         Carteret High that only one black stu-
                         dent turned up for classes--a fifteen-
                         year-old girl named Bettie.

BETTIE TAYLOR: I have to admit that day it was sort of
                         frightening, but it was something that

I felt I had to do. And, ah, you know, I just wasn't backing down.

SAFER: Twenty-one years after Bettie Taylor's enrollment at East Carteret High School, another landmark event: her son Brien enrolled. He wasn't the first at anything, and he wasn't the most popular, and he wasn't the smartest. But he was the one with a 95-mile-an-hour fastball.

Occasionally, it gets up to 98 miles an hour. So fast that if you listen carefully, you can hear it. . . . What [the Yankees] wanted so badly was a six-foot-five, nineteen-year-old lefty, with statistics like these. In some high school games, he would strike out 19 or 20 batters of the 21 he faced. In his last season, he struck out 213 in 88 innings. Nobody ever stole a base on him, because so few ever got on base. He has an arm, his coaches say, is God-given. His career began here in North River, in the littered front yard by the trailer where he grew up, and where the Taylors still live. He developed his arm throwing rocks.

BRIEN TAYLOR: That's all I did. If I wasn't doing some homework sitting at the house, I was out the side of the road throwing rocks.

SAFER: With a very proud grandpa Taylor looking on, looking and listening.

GRANDPA TAYLOR: I'd be standing there looking at him, and I'd be shaking my head, 'cause I'd hear that ball going down there whistling.

SAFER: Whistling?

GRANDPA TAYLOR: Yes sir, making a noise coming down there. I said, My Lord, where did he get that powerful?

SAFER:

His first high school coach, Chuck Lewis, heard that whistling too.

CHUCK LEWIS:

Well, he had that arm, he had that God-given arm that Chuck Lewis had nothing to do with. He walked in the door with it, and all we had to do was channel his mechanics and, and get his head thinking baseball.

SAFER:

There's no way that a talent like that can go unnoticed. It's the stuff that baseball scouts' dreams are made of, and they descended, dozens upon dozens of them, with smiles and shoe-shines, and contracts, and promises, and the thought that there's no way a poor black family can say no to a couple of hundred thousand dollars.
They did not count on Bettie Taylor.

BETTIE TAYLOR:

When they came, they gave me the impression that they had this guy sewed up. You know what I mean? This was a done deal. They . . . they came ready for him to sign papers and everything, you know. Well, they were quite shaken when I told them, no, it's not going to be this way, you know. And I just laid the rules out, and I told them the way it was going to be done, you know.

SAFER:

The Yankees had picked Brien Taylor first in the baseball draft. And when negotiations began, the first thing Bettie Taylor did was to hire a first class lawyer for advice--a city slicker named Scott Boras--who had advised a college player the year before into a 1.2 million dollar signing bonus, the highest ever. Bettie Taylor thought that might be a good place to start.

SAFER:

Smart woman?

SCOTT BORAS:

Very.

SAFER:

Tough?

BORAS: Tough in the sense of rationally tough. She knew what was fair, and she knew to seek a factual basis for her opinions.

SAFER: Bettie Taylor says she made it clear. She wanted Brien to get the same as last year's highest bonus, 1.2 million, and no less. The Yankees countered with an offer of 300 thousand dollars. She said, no.

BETTIE TAYLOR: And I just simply stuck to my guns. I wasn't backing down. I mean, sure, they were the Yankees, you know. Some say the richest organization in baseball. Well, that was no big deal to me. As far as I was concerned, they were just another ball club, and I had something they wanted. So I gave it my best shot.

SAFER: You're a very tough lady.

BETTIE TAYLOR: Well, that was something that I wanted. You know, I mean, this is my kid, you know. Maybe you can push me around, you know, some, but when it comes to the kids, that's a different story. And when you're a mother, you do what you feel you have to do for that child.

SAFER: So they raised it to 650 thousand.

BETTIE TAYLOR: 650 thousand.

SAFER: And you said?

BETTIE TAYLOR: I said, no.

SAFER: It was about then that people in town started wondering if there wasn't something wrong with Bettie Taylor. Maybe she'd shucked a few too many crabs.

SAFER: At the time, did you think she was a little crazy to turn down 600 thousand.

CHUCK LEWIS: Yeah, I said she was crazy.

SAFER: The Yankees wondered as well, and so did
                       a major league scout who had advised the
                       Yankees that Brien would not be hard to
                       sign. He showed up one night at the fam-
                       ily trailer, full of bravado, driving
                       his Mercedes.

BETTIE TAYLOR: Yeah, it was a Mercedes. And he said,
                       wouldn't you like to have a car like
                       this, you know. Well, I mean, anybody in
                       their right mind, you know what's going
                       on there, you know. It sounds to me like
                       it's leading him on, you know. And I told
                       Brien, I said, oh, he's just trying to
                       entice you, you know. So he came and he
                       knocked on the door. And he asked if he
                       could come in. I said, ``No.'' I said,
                       ``I've decided I don't want to talk to
                       you.'' He said, ``But you have to talk.
                       . . ,'' I said, ``No.'' I said, ``I've
                       . . . I've had enough.'' I said, ``I've
                       talked to enough people. I don't want to
                       talk to you.'' He said, ``But if you talk
                       to me . . .'' he said, ``Brien will sign
                       once you've talked to me.'' And I said,
                       ``Well I'm not interested in what you're
                       saying. I don't want to hear it.'' He
                       just simply would not take no for an
                       . . . for an answer. So eventually I
                       told him, I said, ``Well, I don't . . .
                       I wouldn't like to close the door in your
                       face, would you please leave?'' He said,
                       ``Well, that's what you're going to have
                       to do.''

SAFER: And that's what she did. Even though he
                       threatened that baseball would turn its
                       back on Brien Taylor if he didn't sign
                       the contract.

BETTIE TAYLOR: Oh, you talk about conviction, that
                       really did it. That did it. Yeah, he
                       doesn't realize today how much he helped
                       Brien Taylor. He really did.

SAFER: You mean, had the pressure, had they not
                       tried to put the screws to you so much,
                       had they not tried to put so much pres-
                       sure on you, you might have signed for
                       something less?

BETTIE TAYLOR: Oh no.

SAFER: No.

BETTIE TAYLOR: No.

SAFER: The Taylor family motto may well be ''We shall not be moved.'' The Yankees became desperate. Bettie Taylor played to their paranoia with the ultimate threat: no contract. Brien would go to college, which would have stripped the Yankees of their rights to him. They blinked, and came up with an offer of 1.5 million, just to sign a contract. The biggest-ever signing bonus.

SAFER: And you said?

BETTIE TAYLOR: Oh yeah, I'd be a fool not to. I mean, that was even more than what we'd asked for, you know.

SAFER: The Yankees were easy. New York was something else. A zoo of reporters, cameramen, and executives when Brien and Bettie came up to sign. The richest bonus baby in history was in Yankee pin-stripes and a daze.

REPORTER: (NAT SOUND)   Welcome to New York.

SAFER: What was it like walking through there?

BRIEN TAYLOR: Well, it was shocking. It scared me so bad, I went off the end. It was a scary thing, 'cause there was so many people, and I wasn't used to crowds being so big. I mean, they were just hollering. I didn't know what was going on, know what they were saying, or what they were thinking. So many cameras on me, and people talking left and right. It was something I never seen before.

SAFER: You know, you're going to have to get used to that kind of thing?

BRIEN TAYLOR: Yeah.

SAFER: Last October, the Yankees got their first look at Brien Taylor in Florida baseball, in something called the Instructional League. And he's dazzled his new coaches with his talent and his speed.

SAFER: Have you been up at the plate against him?

MAN: Not on your life.

SAFER: Really?

MAN: They don't pay me enough, no.

SAFER: The Yankee coaches are pampering and protecting their investment, convinced that if they bring him along slowly, at least one season in the minor leagues, they'll be once again the Yankees of legend. But there's only so much protecting they can do.

CHUCK LEWIS: I'd worry about things like that, that when he goes . . . after a ballgame, they . . . they . . . the guys go to a bar, or some hangout, and there's pretty girls, and pretty girls after a millionaire, and, ah, he's going to be very popular, and that sort of thing.

SAFER: So far, Brien Taylor, the only millionaire in North River, has been careful with his money. He bought a car, a black Mustang, and his father, Willie Ray, is building their new home right behind the old one.

SAFER: What's it going to be like?

BRIEN TAYLOR: It's a nice house. It's longer than an extra-long trailer, and it's wider than a double-wide.

SAFER: Longer than a . . . than a . . .

BRIEN TAYLOR: Extra-long trailer.

SAFER: Extra-long trailer.

BRIEN TAYLOR: Yeah. And it's wider than a double-wide.

(CHURCH MUSIC)

SAFER: Bettie Taylor likes to say that she put the whole affair in the hands of the Lord, and that it was He who triumphed over the damn Yankees. Bettie followed the Lord, and Brien followed Bettie. So the moral of the story might well be, praise the Lord, but listen to your mother . . . providing, of course, God gave you that arm in the first place.

Note how skillfully Safer and his producer, Jeff Fager, develop the story and bring out the personalities. Bettie Taylor becomes an unforgettable character. Indeed, you come away from this story feeling you know—and like—everyone involved. Safer's words are few, but well chosen. Go back and read where he sets the scene. It's lovely. He uses detail effectively: "Brien's pitches are so fast you can hear 'em."

As we said, a report of this kind is rare in daily television. Time is too precious, and paraphrasing is more efficient. But graceful language and skillful use of detail, as demonstrated by Morley Safer, can enhance everything you write.

As you watch network and local magazine programs you will observe a wide variety of writing styles. That's the beauty of the magazine format. It can include many styles of writing, reporting, and producing. It's interesting work, often coveted by broadcast journalists accustomed to covering only spot news. And because of the popularity of the format, there is likely to be more opportunity to work on these programs in the future.

The stories on "60 Minutes" are minidocumentaries, but regular newscasts often include similar, shorter reports. Producers of these "mini-minis" use the same formula as the producers of standard documentaries. A situation, usually controversial, is presented and opposing views heard. In this example from CNN, the issue is logging in Virginia's George Washington National Forest and what it means in terms of government revenue and jobs. The correspondent is Deborah Potter ("DP" in the transcript), who also wrote the lead-in.

FIRST IT WAS THE SPOTTED OWL, NOW IT'S THE BALANCE SHEET. LOGGERS WORKING IN THE NATIONAL FORESTS ARE UNDER ATTACK AGAIN, NOT FOR ENVIRONMENTAL REASONS, BUT FOR ECONOMICS. DP REPORTS FROM SOUTHWESTERN VIRGINIA:

v/o loggers in the woods   FOR THESE VIRGINIA LOG-GERS, IT'S A LIVING. FOR

	THE FEDERAL TREASURY, IT'S A LOSS. (nat sound)
tree crashes down v/o timber being loaded	THE GOVERNMENT WILL LOSE MONEY ON THE SALE OF THIS TIMBER FROM THE GEORGE WASHINGTON NATIONAL FOREST. AND THERE'S NOTHING UNUSUAL ABOUT IT.
sot: jeffrey olson the wilderness society	Two-thirds of the na- tional forests lose money chronically to the tune of 250-million dollars a year.
v/o trees being hauled out road--with sign or truck	THE FOREST SERVICE CLAIMS THE PROGRAM AS A WHOLE MAKES A HUGE PROFIT. BUT CRITICS SAY THAT'S ONLY BECAUSE THE GOVERNMENT'S POLICY ALLOWS IT TO HIDE ITS REAL COSTS, BY WRITING OFF EXPENSES LIKE ROAD CONSTRUCTION OVER HUNDREDS OF YEARS. THE ACTUAL BOTTOM LINE IS OFTEN IN THE RED.
sot: stephen bennett bennett logging and lumber	It's not that they're subsidizing our indus- try, it's not that they're selling their product too cheap. It just costs them too much money to do business.
sot: rep. jim jontz, d-ind v/o bottom half, aerials	Not even the best man- ager under the best cir- cumstances can make a profit selling timber from some of these for- ests. They are too re- mote, the slopes are too steep, the value of the timber is too low, the growing conditions are

	too difficult. And in those cases I would ar-gue why should we be selling timber below cost.
on camera (tape 3)	WHILE THE FOREST SER-VICE SAYS IT'S MAKING SOME CHANGES, THE NEW POLICY WOULD STILL AL-LOW FOR MONEY-LOSING SALES. BUT THE TIMBER INDUSTRY SAYS THAT PROFIT IS NOT THE ONLY REASON FOR LOGGING IN THE NATIONAL FORESTS.
v/o logging va.	THIS SALE, FOR EXAMPLE, IS DESIGNED TO IMPROVE WILDLIFE HABITAT. OTH-ERS ARE FOR RECREATION OR FOREST MANAGEMENT.
sot: kent robinson national forest products assn	Merely to go after prof-itability may well re-sult in the ill health of the forest and a loss of quality in future stands.
v/o sawmill	EFFORTS IN CONGRESS TO BAN MONEY-LOSING SALES COULD ALSO MEAN A LOSS OF JOBS--UP TO 16-THOU-SAND, ACCORDING TO IN-DUSTRY ESTIMATES. BAD NEWS IN THE WOODS AND SAWMILLS OF SOUTHWEST-ERN VIRGINIA.
sot: jackie smith logger	We cut 90 percent na-tional forest timber so we'd be out of a job. It's our livelihood.
sot: stephen bennett sawmill operator	It's got to affect us. I mean what else is there to do? All we have here is trees.

```
v/o logging--cutting, loading
```

MANY LOGGERS BELIEVE THE ARGUMENT OVER COST IS JUST A PRETEXT TO SILENCE THE SAWS IN ALL THE NATIONAL FORESTS. BUT CRITICS SAY IT MAKES NO SENSE FOR TAXPAYERS TO HAVE TO SUBSIDIZE THE DESTRUCTION OF A PUBLIC RESOURCE--AND UNLESS THE FOREST SERVICE CAN RUN ITS TIMBER SALES LIKE A BUSINESS, THEY SAY, IT SHOULDN'T RUN THEM AT ALL. DP CNN NEAR COVINGTON, VIRGINIA.

The lead-in establishes what the story is about. This will not be the usual environmental report—it's not concerned with the preservation of wildlife, it's about money. (Instead of saying "preservation of wildlife," as she might have, Potter says "spotted owl." She not only says the same thing in half the time, but uses a noun the audience can visualize.) Note the lovely simplicity of the lead: "For these Virginia loggers, it's a living. For the Federal Treasury, it's a loss." No adjectives, no dependent clauses. *Living* and *loss* are not only good nouns, they sound good together. Don't forget sound.

Throughout the piece, words and pictures are in harmony. Viewers, while hearing Potter say, "The government will lose money from the sale of this timber," are looking at a tree being cut down. When she speaks of sawmills, they see a sawmill.

This is a rather complicated story, not easy to tell, and Potter has told it simply and succinctly. It provides an instructive example of tight writing. There is not a word, let alone a sentence, that can be struck without injury to the report.

Specials

An essential part of broadcast journalism is the special. Subject matter may range from the assassination of John F. Kennedy to the destruction of the rain forest in Brazil, but whatever the topic, the radio or television special—like the documentary—demands writing of especially high quality.

Specials blossom when anniversaries are in season. Notable specials marked the twentieth anniversary of the Watergate break-in, the fiftieth anniversary of the attack on Pearl Harbor, and the sixtieth anniversary of Lindbergh's solo flight across the Atlantic. Then there are the so-called "instant specials" produced as events occur—the Election Night specials, for example—and programs produced in the immediate aftermath of events like Hurricane Andrew and the bombing of the World Trade

Center. The writing for these programs is done under great pressure because so much of them will be done live.

Such a special was aired by CNN on the evening of August 21, 1991, when in Moscow the rightist coup collapsed and Mikhail Gorbachev returned to the capital from captivity. Here is how the special, anchored by Bernard Shaw, began that historic night:

```
BERNIE/BOX        (BERNIE)
ANIMATION           THANKS FOR JOINING US.
                    I'M BERNARD SHAW IN
                  WASHINGTON.
                    THIS IS AN HOUR-LONG
                  SPECIAL REPORT ON THE
                  CRISIS IN THE SOVIET UNION.
                    THE COUP IS OVER.
                    MIKHAIL GORBACHEV HAS
                  JUST RETURNED TO MOSCOW . . .
                  NEARLY THREE DAYS AFTER
                  HARDLINERS ANNOUNCED THEY
                  WERE TAKING OVER THE
                  GOVERNMENT.
                    MISTER GORBACHEV'S PLANE
                  TOUCHED DOWN IN MOSCOW
                  ABOUT 45 MINUTES AGO.
TAKE VO           ------VO------
```

Notice the clarity. "This is an hour-long special report on the crisis in the Soviet Union. The coup is over." Each sentence is a simple declarative sentence, starting with the first sentence, "Thanks for joining us." The words themselves are simple, everyday words. And we are dealt one fact at a time. Bernard Shaw says, "During that historic week in the Soviet Union, I found our newswriting exceptionally lean and pointed—requisite writing for reporting historic events."

The World of Sports Writing

The first requirement for sports writing, print or broadcast, is to love sports. If you love sports, live it and sleep it, you will know it. And that's the other major requirement: to know what you're talking about. Sports writers who do not know their subject are—to put it bluntly—dead. And it also helps to know English. To know it well. Too many sportscasters, who may know all they need to know about sports, fail in their efforts because they mutilate the language.

The Washington, D.C. sportscaster Frank Herzog says, "Writing for sports may be one of the most abused and misunderstood areas of broadcast journalism. It requires the usual skills of a journalist—concise statement of fact in easily understandable form. But then the boundaries expand. It calls for a more informal, relaxed, conversational style of writing. And it often includes commentary that is never labeled commentary.'' The style must be able to capture the interest of everyone, not just the sports fan. Stories are not aimed solely at people who love football, baseball, basketball, or hockey. There are considerably more people in the audience.

If you want to get into sports reporting, start in news. Herzog says, ''News reporting establishes a foundation for everything you will do in sports, because good sports reporting starts with coverage of sports as a news story. It is happening. It is affecting the lives of people in the sport and those watching it.''

Another reason for starting in news is that it is much harder to find a small market, entry-level position that involves sports reporting exclusively. It is much more likely that if you are interested in sports, your first job will primarily involve news, although you may have opportunities to anchor sportscasts on weekends and cover some sports events during the week. Positions where you do only sports are more likely to become available after you have been in your first job for a while.

Although most writing and reporting skills are similar in news and sports, there are some skills that are more critical in sports reporting. Once you are familiar with the various sports, the teams, and the participants, you will be expected to use that knowledge to write and report under the most severe of deadlines. Often you'll be on the air with a sports report while other games are in progress and scores are changing. Frequently your script will show only the scores—final or otherwise—and you will have to fill in details extemporaneously. You might have to explain, without the comfort of a script, that the score was tied on a pinch hit home run in the bottom the ninth, or that it was the team's seventh straight win, that the starting pitcher failed for the third time to get his twentieth win, or that the player who scored the winning touchdown had just been traded from one team to the other.

You get the picture. Ideally, you would have time to put this kind of detail in your script, but in covering sports it's often necessary to base your report on prior knowledge and a sketchy listing of the details of the game. You'll need to have a grasp of these details and be able to think and speak well on your feet.

The broadcast industry is becoming more and more interested in sportscasters who are writers and reporters—good writers and good reporters. And although the industry still insists on using some former jocks as sports reporters, largely because of their name recognition value, those who have been successful as sportscasters have had to prove that—in addition to being recognized—they had developed the needed writing and reporting skills.

Much of the best sports writing isn't limited to local sportscasts or to cable networks specializing in sports. Dick Schaap is an ABC reporter whose work shows up in productions of both ABC News and ABC Sports. Schaap has a way of bringing out the human side in sports stories, using the tools of broadcast journalism to tell compelling sports stories.

This report, by Schaap, was aired on ABC's "World News Sunday" on December 22, 1991. Note how it uses a powerful combination of audio and video.

SCHAAP--THE NEW SHOE

CLOSE-UP OF SHOEMAKER PULL BACK TO SHOW HIM IN WHEELCHAIR	Some people said Bill Shoemaker was the greatest *athlete* they ever saw. Many said no, just the greatest rider. He's sixty now, and still riding--a wheel chair, a constant reminder of the terrible auto crash last spring that left him a quadriplegic, every jockey's nightmare.
CINDY, HIS WIFE: (on brink of tears)	It's amazing, He shouldn't be here. And he fought, very, very hard. I'm very proud of him.
BILL SHOEMAKER:	I thought about being paralyzed a lot of times, and I didn't want to go through it, no. But now that it has happened, and I've kind of gotten used to it. . . .
SHOEMAKER IN BARNS	Bill Shoemaker is back at work--in the barns at dawn, training horses, studying horses.
SHOEMAKER (VO):	You can look in their eyes as they walk by and tell whether they're feeling good or feeling bad, or ready to go or not ready.
SHOEMAKER WITH HORSE	No one ever had a better feel for a horse. Now Shoe has no feeling from the neck down. He also feels no bitterness.
SHOEMAKER:	Things happen to you, some of 'em you like, some of 'em you don't like, but I'll beat this thing. I can move my hands a little bit now.
SCHAAP WITH CINDY AND FAMILY	Shoemaker has his hopes and his horses . . . and his family.

CINDY SHOEMAKER:	This is the hand that he's been dealt and he'll play it.
SCHAAP:	And the same for you?
CINDY:	I'd love to throw the cards back in, but you can't so we just go on.
SHOEMAKER IN WHEEL-CHAIR	Once Shoemaker was a sorcerer in a saddle, a tiny man guiding massive animals through narrow treacherous openings, winning more than eight hundred races, more than any other rider. Now he guides a massive wheelchair, a puff and sip, it is called. By inhaling or exhaling, Shoe can move forward or back, take the lead or lay off the pace.
CINDY:	I know he's always working, always testing himself.
SCHAAP:	It must be in many ways, as great a challenge as manipulating a big horse.
SHOEMAKER:	It's probably more of a challenge, but it's fun doing it.
SHOEMAKER IN WHEEL-CHAIR	For Shoemaker, challenges have always been grim fun. He never gloated in victory, never whined in defeat.
SCHAAP:	In some ways, do you appreciate life more?
SHOEMAKER:	I do, sure. Yes, I do. Just being able to come out here and watch my horses and train them and then have them run good once in a while, that's a great feeling.
CINDY:	I'm very blessed that I still have him. I could've ended up with a man who had the use of his body and had no brain.
CINDY PUSHING WHEELCHAIR	Sometimes Cindy gives Shoe a little help.

SHOEMAKER:	I'll wind up in the pool.
SCHAAP:	Shoe has not lost his quiet sense of humor. He used to be a golf addict. When you do get back on the golf course, you'll get more strokes for this.
SHOEMAKER:	I should, although one of my friends, Pierce, has said, I'm not giving you any strokes. (SMILES) Dead even. (BIG SMILE)

FREEZE ON BIG SMILE

Through a combination of writing and reporting skills, strong video, sensitive questions, and editing with an artist's touch, Schaap has created a sports story that could easily compete with the best network news story. Note the effective blending of Shoemaker's life as a jockey and as a quadriplegic: "He's sixty now, and still riding—a wheelchair." And: "No one ever had a better feel for a horse. Now Shoe has no feeling from the neck down."

Here is another Schaap script, this from "ABC World News Tonight," aired on October 23, 1991, during the World Series between the Atlanta Braves and the Minnesota Twins.

SCHAAP--STOP THE
   CHOP?

INDIAN BEATS DRUM/ CHANTS	They marched to different drummers . . . the small band of native Americans who demonstrated their anger outside the stadium last night,
BRAVES FANS BEATING ON DRUMS & CHANTING	and the thousands of Braves fans who demonstrated their delight . . . who put on war paint and headdresses and swung tomahawks to celebrate the first World Series game ever played in Atlanta.
CLYDE BELLECOURT, INDIAN:	We're challenging you to get rid of these tomahawks, the ugly paint on your faces, to get rid of those chicken feathers.
HECKLER YELLS:	Nobody is making fun of you. Nobody is making fun of you.

FANS AND INDIANS	The Indians say they *are* being made fun of, are being stereotyped, portrayed as savages. They say it is demeaning and racist to use a race of people as *mascots*. They've already had an impact. A week ago Ted Turner, who owns the team, and his fiancee, Jane Fonda, who used to champion Indian causes, were doing the tomahawk chop, a ritual during Braves games. But in response to the protests, Ted and Jane have stopped.
JIMMY CARTER:	I'll be doing the tomahawk chop. You watch Wednesday night.
SCHAAP:	Former President Jimmy Carter says the chop is a compliment to Indians.
CARTER:	This is a brave, courageous, successful team, and I think we can look upon American Indians as brave, successful, and attractive.
ANDREW YOUNG, FORMER ATLANTA MAYOR	I see it as a respect for native American culture.
SCHAAP:	It's sort of like The Fighting Irish. It never hurt Notre Dame.
AARON TWO ELK:	But you don't see people dressing up as priests and nuns and, every time they score a touchdown or hit a home run, sprinkling holy water on a drunk.
SCHAAP:	Not all native Americans are offended.
INDIAN:	Here in Cherokee we're all rooting for the Braves . . .
SCHAAP:	The Indians of Cherokee, North Carolina, have a vested interest.
INDIAN CONTINUES:	. . . we don't find it degrading.
SCHAAP:	They make tomahawks and headdresses that are selling well in Atlanta

these days--to the dismay of pro-
testers.

KEN RHYNES, INDIAN: There's always what we call hang-
around-the-fort Indians.

SCHAAP: Clearly, most of the Braves' fans are
not trying to *offend*. They're trying
to have fun.

INDIAN: But it's not funny to us.

SCHAAP: Just as clearly, some people *are* of-
fended, and they feel they've found
a perfect time to spark a dialogue.
Dick Schaap, ABC News, Atlanta.

This could just as well be called a news story. It's related to a sports event, but the story deals with a topic that is as much at home in a newscast as in a sportscast. In fact, as we mentioned, this was carried on "World News Tonight," ABC's nightly network newscast. We repeat: the basics are the same. The skills that make a successful broadcast newswriter also make a successful sportswriter.

Dick Schaap said, "It is much more important to be clear than clever." And he is right. Above all else, his sports reporting is clear and compelling.

One final thought: don't become one of those sports reporters who refuses to use the same verb twice when giving the nightly list of scores. If you constantly have winning teams whipping, trouncing, triumphing, overwhelming, thrashing, devastating, crushing, or even murdering the losers, you are taking extra time to write something that takes extra time to read. Plus, you're distracting your audience. Simple words like "win" or "defeat" not only do just fine, they wear well. This is not to say you should never use *whip, trounce,* or *crush.* Just think about how your sportscast sounds. Don't strain. Be conversational. Cardinal rules for all broadcast newswriters.

Commentary

You may never be a commentator, although stations and networks always have carried sports commentary as well as political commentary, and, of course, military commentary upon occasions such as the Gulf War. Because much of the best broadcast writing appears in commentaries, you can learn from studying them. It usually is copy written by journalists known for their writing ability as well as good judgment.

Perhaps you will write essays, which can be almost indistinguishable from commentary. Here are examples of both. Study them for structure, noting how the words, phrases, clauses, and sentences are assembled. Then study them for clarity, for flow of language, for the use—or non-use—of adjectives, and for the choice of nouns and verbs. Read them aloud. You will find it a pleasurable experience. Good writing has such a good sound.

We start with the commentary—essay?—Eric Sevareid wrote when Ed Murrow died.

> This is not a normal day in this establishment. None of us here has worked easily or well. It is a day we knew was coming but for which we could not properly prepare, try as we would.
>
> It is not my privilege to speak for all of Ed Murrow's colleagues, and it is not possible for me to speak even for myself as I would wish to speak. One day someone may find the right words. There are some of us here—and I am one—who owe their professional life to this man. There are many working here and at other networks and stations who owe to Ed Murrow their love of their work, their standards, their sense of responsibility.
>
> I never knew any person among those who worked in his realm to feel jealousy toward him, not only because he made himself a refuge for those in trouble, a source of strength for those who were weak, but because there was no basis for comparison. He was an original, and we shall not see his like again. He was an artist, passionately alive, living each day as if it were his last, absorbing and radiating the glories and miseries of his generation—the men, the machines, the battles, the beauties.
>
> The poetry of America was in his bones. He believed in his family, his friends, his work and his country. Himself he often doubted. Next to his own land he loved England the best. Their people owe him much. I would presume to use the words of England's greatest poet about another brave and brooding figure who also died too young: "Goodnight, sweet prince."

To dissect such an essay would be a desecration. Sevareid said that one day someone might find the right words. After studying what he wrote one feels that he found them.

It may be that of all radio and television commentaries the one Walter Cronkite delivered on the futility of continuing the Vietnam War is best remembered. In a CBS News special on February 27, 1968, he said:

> To say that we are closer to victory today is to believe, in the face of the evidence, the optimists who have been wrong in the past. To suggest we are on the edge of defeat is to yield to unreasonable pessimism. To say that we are mired in a stalemate seems the only realistic, yet unsatisfactory solution. On the off chance that military and political analysts

are right, in the next few months we must test the enemy's intentions in case this [the Tet offensive] is indeed his last big gasp before negotiations. But it is increasingly clear to this reporter that the only rational way out then will be to negotiate, not as victors, but as an honorable people who lived up to their pledge to defend democracy and did the best they could.

How, for television, do you write an indictment of the president of the United States? This is the commentary that Howard K. Smith wrote for ABC's evening news in the aftermath of Watergate. The date was October 31, 1973.

President Nixon has put a strain on the nation's trust that is nearly unbearable.

We were told aide John Dean was uncovering the truth about Watergate. It turned out he was doing the opposite. We were told John Ehrlichman was. It turned out he wasn't. We were told Special Prosecutor Cox was being allowed to. As we know, he was not.

Now today the sudden revelation that two important tapes of conversations, promised to the court, do not exist. That deepens suspicions inevitably that there has been a cover-up all along and it is still going on.

In the meantime, blow upon unprecedented blow has been dealt us. Two of the President's former cabinet secretaries indicted, a horde of high aides resigning under pressure, some of them also indicted. The latest attorney general and his deputy out for promising an independent investigation. And—though not directly related, it weighs in the balance—a twice-chosen Vice-President out for plain corruption.

I think it is not excessive to say we have been put through too much. Either the Congress, or the President by his own decision, should relieve us of a burden too heavy to carry any longer.

The somber language is in keeping with the gravity of the situation. Note the solemnity of the short declarative sentences in the second, third, and fourth paragraphs. One senses that Smith, with some sadness, is saying what he felt duty-bound to say.

Network commentary languished in the 1980s. We no longer heard Howard K. Smith, Eric Sevareid, or Frank Reynolds. Only NBC's John Chancellor came on the evening news with comment. But in the early 1990s, commentary experienced a small revival. This was noticeable on the weekends, when network correspondents like Garrick Utley of NBC and Bruce Morton of CBS interpreted the news.

When the Soviet Union collapsed, Morton wrote an essay summarizing its three-quarter-century experiment with communism in just two minutes. Even so, it could have been tedious. Summaries usually are. But because of words chosen and the way they were arranged, it was exciting. Here is most of what Morton wrote:

Vladimir Illich Lenin made a revolution and dreamed a dream. He would make a new man, Soviet man, caring, communal, and good. What he did was make a big new country. It lasted 74 years.

Big deeds, always, good or evil. Joseph Stalin may have killed a million people collectivizing farms in the Ukraine. That is a number; nobody really knows. Ten million, they say, died in the camps. Lately, we have begun to recover their bones. But that is just a number. Nobody really knows.

The big new country built some muscles, made iron and steel. It fought Hitler's Germans on a scale the rest of us cannot imagine. Twenty million died in the Great Patriotic War, they say. Every city has its monument. Every family had its dead. The big new country hurled a beeping globe into space, and the United States, which thought it was the scientific king of the hill, shook in its shoes. Nikita Khrushchev thundered he would bury us. We listened nervously.

In the end, the big new country failed on little things. Couldn't deliver a side of beef. Soviet man—usually Soviet woman—spent a life waiting in line for goods that never came. Leonid Brezhnev's bureaucrats dozed, fat and happy—goodies, always, for themselves while the country sickened. . . . Finally, somebody whispered, "Freedom," and the whole weird place came tumbling down.

Whether you are a student or a professional, surely you would like to have written that. Note the devices used: the strong verbs—*hurled, shook, thundered*—the repetition of *big new country* and *nobody really knows,* and the sensitivity to sound—"have begun to recover their bones." Through artistry Morton succeeded in making the familiar seem fresh.

One of broadcasting's most televised incidents must be the beating of Rodney King by the Los Angeles police. Because of the videotape, conviction of the black man's attackers seemed certain. Instead, they were acquitted in the trial involving state charges,* and the acquittal caused Andy Rooney of "60 Minutes" to forsake his role of amusing curmudgeon and to speak out strongly on what he saw as violation of one of this country's most basic principles—equality before the law. His highly personal approach contrasts sharply with the historical vignette composed by Morton. This is how, forthrightly, Rooney ended his essay:

In the 1960s, when blacks were still sitting in the back of the bus, the overwhelming majority of American men and women were in favor of every anti-discrimination law that was passed by Congress. They believed in equality before the law even if they privately felt superior to the guy over on the other side of town. Even people who were prejudiced and discriminatory in their personal lives . . . you know, belonged to

_____
*They were convicted later on lesser federal charges.

clubs that didn't accept blacks or preferred to live in all-white neighbor-hoods . . . even these people were fair enough and good enough to understand that before the law in our country, everyone should be treated the same. And that's the tragedy of this Rodney King case. This one black man didn't get fair and equal treatment under our law.

It's depressing and sad for all of us. I feel worst for the majority of black people in America, the ones the television cameras didn't see, the ones who when the decision was announced, didn't riot. They put their black faces in their black hands and wept.

In Conclusion

Commentary is a form of journalism to be practised by men and women of experi-ence because it is often the most controversial writing you can do. Some people are impatient to be commentators. They want, on finishing college, to go out and express their opinions right away. That's a mistake. The qualifications to pass judgment—to analyze and appraise—must be earned. And when you *do* do it, be sure you have done your homework. If you do not know the facts and lack perspective, you will be a broadcaster without honor in your own shop and, very soon, in every place you may be heard.

14. *Your Electronic Link to the World: The News Services*

Much of the news we hear on the air comes from one or more of the major press associations, such as the Associated Press, Although there are competing domestic and international services, the AP is the dominant service in the United States.

Some stations, regrettably, have come to depend entirely on the news gathered by one of these services. As good as that service may be, these stations default on their responsibility to cover local developments. Ever since broadcast stations were largely deregulated by the federal government, some local stations have discontinued covering local news. However, in many markets, one or more stations have answered this trend by *expanding* their local coverage to better serve the audience's need.

Since this chapter—indeed, this entire text—is written for newswriters, it is not relevant to those stations where staff announcers routinely take news from the service, sit down before a microphone, and read. Its only relevance for these "rip and read" stations may be that it perhaps shows them to what degree, in this respect, their reporting is inadequate.

What the Services Provide

The major press associations provide a variety of services. It is helpful to understand these services. We will summarize some of the primary services offered by the Associated Press because most stations are AP subscribers. Bear in mind that options vary with different services. The news is distributed by satellite to newsroom computers or printers.

1. The basic broadcast wire, called AP NewsPower, carries news, sports, business, and agriculture news, entertainment news and features, and weather. The stories are written in broadcast style, packaged for news and sports programming, and transmitted to the station's newsroom computer system or to a teletype machine. These include news headlines and longer, in-depth stories, which are transmitted during the morning and afternoon drive times.
2. Other services, called AP Drive Time and APHeadlines, are intended for those stations with a smaller appetite for news. They include one-minute summaries, along with a modest amount of sports, business, and weather information. They also include all late-breaking news bulletins.
3. Premium services, such as AP NewsTalk, are intended for television stations and for news-intensive radio stations. NewsTalk includes the complete NewsPower package, plus complete newspaper wire versions of stories that also move on the broadcast wire. AP MegaStream is a service intended primarily for the broadcast networks. In addition to the other premium services, this package includes various state and regional wires from throughout the country.
4. Audio services, such as live and taped news reports, are provided around the clock by AP and its competitors. Among these are complete newscasts (including ''windows'' into which local stations may insert commercials), actualities, voice reports, and specialized audio packages in areas such as entertainment, business, and sports.

These services are available to stations and networks at a price. Only the networks and the largest stations can afford to subscribe to all, or most, of them. Smaller stations generally subscribe to more limited services, often only the basic broadcast wire.

Wire services depend heavily on their subscribing broadcast stations, and newspapers, to provide them with material. Thus the stories that you receive from a wire service will have been written, and rewritten, by a variety of writers working for local media outlets or for the wire service itself, or both. These multiple sources make it especially important for the local broadcast writer to rewrite wire copy so as to relate it to local stories or angles.

Some radio networks provide their own versions of wire services for their affiliates. For example, ABC News Wire is a satellite-delivered service providing national and international news culled from Reuters, the British press association, and Gannett News Media, which uses the resources of *USA Today* and the Gannett News Service. Also, CBS services its affiliates with Zapnews, a variety of daily news and information packages delivered by computer and linked to audio reports carried over the CBS radio networks.

Television stations, in addition to choosing from these options, can also receive video and audio reports through closed circuit "newsfeeds." These stories are packaged and distributed by satellite by a variety of producers and syndicators, including NBC News Channel, CBS's Newsnet, and CNN's Newsource. Stations, regardless of network affiliation, can subscribe to Conus, a kind of television news cooperative that gathers stories from its subscribing stations and then distributes them to other national or regional subscribers. Conus, based in St. Paul, Minnesota, provides live feeds of breaking news events in addition to a regular schedule of newsfeeds to its more than one hundred subscribers.

Organizing and Using Wire Copy

The task of using wire copy is going to take two quite different forms, depending on whether your newsroom uses a computer system. Your job will be greatly simplified if your station uses AP's NewsDesk or similar computer system. Such systems can store all wire service and local stories and retain your newscast formats. Some adjust for your reading rate, and a number of them include an atlas, a pronunciation guide, and a thesaurus. They permit much easier electronic editing than the traditional process for hard copy.

However, since many newsrooms still are not computerized, it is important to understand the basics of coping with wire copy (or how "not to let the wire copy get the best of you"). Especially if your station subscribes to one of the more copy intensive services, you must have a system for organizing your wire copy so as not to be overwhelmed by sheer mass of material.

We offer some suggestions on handling wire copy if your newsroom does not have the convenience of a computer system that includes your wire service. Every writer has a different way of handling copy. These, however, are the basics:

Use a ruler to tear your stories. If you use scissors, you are wasting time.

Discard all stories you *know* you won't use. Exercise editorial judgment. If you don't winnow out the less newsworthy stories at this stage, you will have an unmanageable accumulation of wire copy by the time you start to write. And remember that stories keep coming as you write. You must keep up with them.

File all stories—"backgrounders"—you may need for future reference. These are stories perhaps outlining campaign issues, summarizing Supreme Court decisions, listing new members of the president's or the governor's cabinet, identifying the states that made up the former Soviet Union, etc. Throw away such a story today and, inevitably, you will wish you had it tomorrow.

Plan how you will arrange copy on your desk. One system would be to place all Washington stories you may use in your next newscast in one pile, all other domestic stories in another pile, all European dateline stories in another pile, and so forth. The whole purpose is to give you easy access to a news story when you want it. Easy access means time saved.

Label your stories. Make your labels as brief as possible, again to save time. Print your slugs—labels—in capital letters so they stand out. Some writers do this in felt-tipped pens for easy identification. There is no rule except to handle your copy efficiently.

Make a list of your stories. You have read them superficially, enough to know you did not want to throw them away. You must decide which of these stories will go into your newscast. Which are most important, most interesting as of that hour? The list will help you decide. The next step is to make a new list, arranging the stories in the order they will be reported.

You'll usually group together those stories that are related. That is, it is logical to go from a story on a political crisis in France to one on the death of a government leader in Germany. An unusual development in the weather or a surprising economic report can lead naturally to wrap-ups in your script on what is happening, more generally, regarding the weather or economics. Similarly, it's proper to wrap together reports coming from a specific geographic area, such as Eastern Europe or the Far East. For example, news from Hong Kong, Beijing, and Tokyo may be reported together in a sort of Far East package.

Even with this list, which amounts to an outline, you are still not ready to start writing. You must find out—from your news director, producer, or news editor—which of these stories will be covered by a reporter on videotape, or, if you are in radio, on audio tape. If a reporter is covering a story, you will need to write a lead-in, introducing the story and the reporter. You will need to know exactly what is in the report. Has there been a late development since the reporter filed the report? Is there a portion of the story omitted in the report? If so, it will be up to you to cover the new development or the missing angle in your script. So it is important for *you* to view the reports and listen to the audio tapes before you write.

And, of course, you must give the wire copy—the raw material from which you must write—a close reading.

Reading Wire Copy

Learn to read copy from a news service critically. If it says something that appears illogical, or doesn't sound right to you in any way, *question it*. Don't automatically accept it. A poor explanation for an illogical statement in your script is "Well, that's what the wire says." News directors and editors have little patience with that excuse. If it sounds illogical to you, it will sound illogical to your listeners.

Here's an example. A wire service reported a "leveling" of the cost of living. It based this generalization on the fact that for two consecutive months the cost of living had risen by four-tenths of 1 percent. The reasoning was wrong. What the statistics really meant was that, instead of leveling off, the cost of living was *increasing at a constant rate*. The wire service writer had come to an erroneous conclusion, and an alert editor fortunately discovered the mistake. But a newswriter could have easily accepted the statement at face value. You need to read wire service copy critically. Be skeptical of what you read on the wire. Always ask yourself, "Does this make sense?"

Remember that the story you are reading is the product of someone who, like yourself, is capable of human error. That person's judgment must be subject to review by you, no matter how high the service's batting average may be in this regard. Do not assume that, because a story comes to you from a wire service, it is somehow endowed with infallibility. News agencies do commit errors. That is why, as soon as errors are discovered, they file corrections.

Another warning. You must catch such corrections as soon as they move on the wire. Reading through the mass of wire service copy and tearing the stories, you can easily miss a correction. If you do, your story perpetuates the mistake, compounding it as a large audience listens. And before you call a wire service regarding a mistake, check the wire carefully to see if it has moved a correction. It's embarrassing to call and be told that a correction has already moved. It means you haven't been alert.

But do not hesitate to call if a *significant* mistake appears to have been made. (Don't bother the wire service about typos!) Feel free to query your local, state, or regional bureau. If the bureau doesn't have an answer for you by airtime, skip the story if you can. Or perhaps you can omit that part of the story which is questionable.

If your station has its own reporter on the scene, of course that is whom you should call. And "go" with what your reporter tells you. A reporter won't be wrong often and still be around!

All right, you say, but what if you have no reporter who covered the story? And what if your wire service doesn't make clear what happened? And what if you have struck out in your telephone call to the wire service bureau? What then?

Under these circumstances, no sure formula exists for getting the information, except to be resourceful. Turn reporter yourself. Call the office or home of the person or persons involved to supplement, or clarify, the information in wire stories. That's fairly common practice. When faced with a confusing wire service story about a standoff between police and a kidnapping suspect, a resourceful local writer telephoned an office overlooking the site of the standoff and asked a secretary to describe what she could see out her window. It was a simple, yet creative way to check out a confusing story and get an eyewitness account.

It is important to remember that wire service stories that move shortly after an event may contain preliminary—in some cases unverified—information. A bulletin may say twenty persons died in a bus accident in New Jersey, but the next version may quote an official saying fifteen died. A later version may quote a police officer saying there were eighteen fatalities. Which do you choose? In this case, it would be safe to say "at least fifteen people died" in the bus accident, taking the lowest figure. You may also say that one report places the death toll as high as twenty. You don't have to choose just one figure. Level with your listeners. Let them know the figures are preliminary and that they vary.

Advisories

In reading wire service copy, always pay close attention to advisories as well as corrections. The advisories can be crucial in writing a story. They may inform you, for example, that an important speech that had been marked for 6:30 P.M. release is now for immediate release because someone, somewhere, broke the embargo. If you are preparing a 6 P.M. newscast, this information enables you to go ahead and write the story. You may want to make it your lead.

Advisories can also tell you about hearings that have been canceled or about news conferences that will—or will not—be held. Or the advisory may simply say, "So-and-so will meet with reporters in the west lobby immediately after today's swearing-in ceremony." Usually the advisory tells you the time and place where the meeting will occur. Besides helping you plan the content of upcoming newscasts, by letting you know a certain story will be breaking, it helps your station to arrange coverage.

An advisory may tell you that the NCAA basketball champions have a 3 P.M. appointment with the president, and that photographs can be taken in the Rose Garden at 3:10. Another advisory may say that a White House statement on joint space exploration is expected momentarily. In other words, stand by for a new story. If you have already written a story on the subject, it may have to be revised. (Remember that news never stops. Stories often have to be updated, even as you write.)

Kill any story that the wire service commands you to kill. Such stories often are incorrect, or loaded with libel. Whatever the problem, you want none of it.

Bulletins

The wire services precede major late-breaking stories with words such as *Flash, Bulletin,* or *Urgent.* The *flash* is rarely seen. It is reserved for news of transcendent importance, such as the death of the president. *Bulletin* matter is more common. First reports of an airline disaster will be bulletined; so will the final score of a championship game, *Urgent* is still more common; it signifies that the wire service regards the story as more than routine.

In broadcast journalism, "bulletin" treatment is accorded a story much less often than on the wires. The wire bulletin interrupts the flow of other news. The station or network bulletin frequently interrupts other programming. Unless a news program is in progress, most bulletin material is saved until the next newscast, usually within the hour. On all-news radio, of course, the wire service bulletin goes on the air at once.

The "Skeds"

Early each morning the wire services file their schedules, or "skeds," listing the major stories the wires will be carrying throughout the day. The schedules consist of brief summaries of stories expected to be filed. They also estimate how long each story will be. They are, in effect, the menus of the news to be served by the agencies to you, their client, and they are of obvious benefit in helping you plan your newscasts. They tell you not only what stories will be moved, but also which stories they believe will be most important. The first story listed is deemed, in their judgment, to be the lead story. On this, quite naturally, wire services do not always agree. Nor do you need to agree with them. But these schedules—or "budgets," as they are sometimes called—do show you the thinking of some of the country's top editors, and their thoughts should be valuable to you in making your own editorial judgments.

So when the skeds come in, save them to refer to.

Study the Copy Thoroughly

Studying the copy takes time. Whether you are scrolling through stories on your computer terminal or reading copy fresh off your printer, you feel the pressure to finish your script, and every minute counts. But unless you are working right up against a deadline, and the newscast is about to go on the air, you should read *every word* of the wire service story. Resist the temptation to start writing after the first four or five paragraphs, when you *think* you know what it's all about. Read the copy all the way through. It takes only a little longer. The writer for the wire service may have buried an important fact—a fascinating angle—in the last few lines.

Even a bulletin cannot always be accepted "as is." Press associations compete with each other to get their bulletin matter out first. Because of this competition, this rush, they do not always take time to place the new development in perspective. You must do this when you rewrite the bulletin for broadcast. For example, when the United States launched an air attack on Iraq on January 17, 1991, the first wire service bulletin made no direct reference to the Iraqi takeover of Kuwait, which had occurred five and one-half months earlier. Experienced newswriters knew at once— without waiting for "adds" on the press association wire—that the two stories were related. They recognized the new incident as another step in the escalation of hostilities in the area, dating back to the 1990 Iraqi invasion of Kuwait. So they might have written this, tying the two angles together:

> Here is a bulletin from the newsroom. The United States and its allies have gone to war against Iraq. Just minutes ago, the U-S began to

attack Baghdad with wave after wave of fighter-bombers and cruise missiles after fruitlessly demanding for five-and-one-half months that Iraq withdraw from Kuwait. Operation Desert Storm—the Pentagon's code name for the war—began less than 24 hours after the U-N deadline for Iraqi President Saddam Hussein to withdraw his forces.

Such treatment of a bulletin is not editorializing—it's good news judgment. There is a world of difference between expressing editorial opinion and placing news in its context. Thus writers are editors not only because of what they omit in the broadcast version of a story but also because of what, on occasion, they add.

Not every story, of course, needs backgrounding. The test is whether significance is lost when background is left out.

Another reason for careful scrutiny of wire copy is libel. One service used this lead:

LOS ANGELES—A MOTORIST-SNIPER WHO TERRORIZED THE SOUTHWEST AREA OF THE CITY WHEN HE WOUNDED THREE PERSONS IN A PRE-DAWN ATTACK WEDNESDAY SURRENDERED MEEKLY TO OFFICERS AT HIS ATTIC HIDEAWAY TODAY.

This is clearly libelous. The wire service has convicted the man without benefit of a trial. What if he was *not* the motorist-sniper who wounded three persons? And even if he was, the wire service had no business convicting him. That is up to the courts.

So *study* the copy as it scrolls on your screen or comes from your printer. Examine it for accuracy, for possible libel, for "holes," essential facts that somehow may have been missed.

And study it so you will have in your mind all the basic elements of the story you are about to rewrite. When you have read the wire copy carefully, set it aside and *tell* the story in your own words. *Talk* it into your computer or your typewriter. Refer to the wire copy only to check details, such as numbers and the spelling of proper names. It's not a bad idea to circle names, figures, and dates when you are going through the copy. Some newswriters also do a considerable amount of underlining, but don't underline so much that it loses its usefulness.

Tell the story as you would tell a person who just asked you what just happened downtown, in Congress, or in the Middle East.

Copying Wire Copy

Students often ask how much of a wire story they can copy. They ask "What if the AP says it better than I can? Why not use their language? Aren't we paying for it?"

Yes, you are paying for it. And if the wire service reports a fact simply and succinctly, certainly it is no crime to use the same wording. But in most cases to copy what the wire service has written is wrong. Not only is some of the copy written mainly for newspapers, but often the story is much longer than your story will be. Your job is to tell the story in a shorter, more lucid form.

Beware of copying the "cute" phrase. During a strike by London garbage collectors, the AP used "A Buckingham Palace spokesman sniffed that court officials had no idea how the royal garbage problem was going to be solved." This cutie wasn't worth copying, but even if it were, it still shouldn't be. Any piece of especially clever writing in wire service copy is apt to be aired by stations across the country. Worse still, it often is repeated in later newscasts. The phrase, original when the wire service writer wrote it, becomes hackneyed within hours. And it could be within minutes, if the phrase appears on the broadcast wire.

As a general rule, don't copy. It's rare that you cannot improve on wire service language, and news directors like their newscasts to be different from every other newscast in the area. They all, of course, want their newscasts to be the best.

For you, too, it should be a matter of pride.

The Broadcast Wire

The basic broadcast wire carries stories that in most cases are already rewritten to be read on the air. So our advice on copying applies less to this wire, although you should continue to read the stories with a critical eye, and you may want—indeed, need—to do some rewriting.

Generally, stories on the broadcast wire are much shorter than stories on the newspaper wire. Because most stations rely heavily or exclusively on the broadcast wires, it is these abbreviated stories that are heard most frequently. They obviously play an important role in local broadcast journalism.

Let's take a specific example. The 1991 U.S. assault on Iraq ended quickly. Known as the Gulf War, this carefully orchestrated military attack lasted six weeks—and only four days once the U.S.–led ground offensive began. This was the main Associated Press story for afternoon newspapers on February 28, announcing the end of the war:

> The battlefields of the Persian Gulf were quiet today. Saddam Hussein's Iraq, broken by a six-week beating in the air and on the ground, bowed to all allied demands and hewed to the cease-fire announced by President Bush.
>
> World leaders and ordinary Americans alike hailed the cease-fire that appeared to herald the end of the Persian Gulf War and turned to the sober task of reckoning its costs in blood, money, and hatred. . . .
>
> At least 126 allied troops were killed in the war. Seventy-nine Americans were killed in action, including 28 in the ground war. Another 28 Americans died in an Iraqi scud attack on a barracks in Saudi Arabia.
>
> Iraqi casualties were far, far higher, with one estimate ranging up

to 100,000 dead and wounded. Allied commanders have refused to provide any count of Iraqi war dead, and Iraq has issued none so far.

Continuation of the cease-fire was contingent on a halt to Iraqi attacks—in the war zone or with missiles—and other conditions including the immediate release of prisoners of war and any captured civilians.

Despite bellicose claims of victory by Baghdad radio, the Iraqi army was in shambles today, decimated by the allies' lightning four-day offensive and the withering 5½-week air assault that preceded it.

The allies destroyed, captured, or otherwise defeated 42 Iraqi divisions, leaving only one full division intact.

The fighting reached its peak Wednesday, as allied armies recaptured Kuwait City and lanced to within 150 miles of Baghdad.

"There was nothing between us and Baghdad," said Operation Desert Storm commander Gen. H. Norman Schwarzkopf. He said the allies could have walked into the Iraqi capital unmolested but had no intention of capturing Iraq.

Iraq's best forces were devastated in what was billed as the biggest tank battle since World War II.

Note that these first paragraphs of the newspaper story contain considerable current detail mixed with occasional references to the background and context of the story. The treatment, even this portion of it, is probably longer than most broadcast stations would use. The story includes a number of words and phrases that, although not very conversational, are quite acceptable in a comprehensive story such as this—words and phrases such as *hewed, herald the end of the . . . war,* and *the sober task of reckoning its cost. . . .* It's effective writing, appropriate for longer newspaper formats, but does not fit the needs of most broadcasters.

A broadcast wire would handle such a story differently. The story would be rewritten in a shorter, more focused, more conversational style. It would be ready to be read on the air. And it would likely sound something like this:

The six-week Gulf War is over.

Iraq's leader, Saddam Hussein, has agreed to all allied demands including an immediate cease-fire.

The agreement ends six weeks of warfare and four days of ground war. The fighting claimed 107 American lives, while estimates of Iraqi casualties run as high as 100-thousand.

Even though Baghdad radio has claimed victory, the Iraqi army is in a shambles. The allies destroyed, captured or defeated 42 of Iraq's 43 military divisions.

The commander of Operation Desert Storm, General Norman Schwarzkopf, said the allies could have walked into Baghdad unmolested, but that conquering Iraq was never the goal.

Compare these versions of the same story. You should be able to see the different writing styles and amount of detail. For example, the broadcast version adds together the 79 Americans killed in action and the 28 killed in their barracks for one casualty total of 107. The shorter version is adequate for the formats of most radio stations. However, stations with an all-news or news-talk format probably will want to receive the longer newspaper version of such stories. These stations subscribe to at least one more comprehensive service that includes both broadcast and newspaper wires.

A Burst of Access

There has been an explosion in computer-assisted journalism. In computerized newsrooms the writer benefits, not only from word processing, electronic editing (audio and video), and story storage and retrieval, but also from a ready access to information only dreamed of a few years ago. Dialog Information Services provides electronic access to millions of articles from newspapers and magazines. Visnews has similar archival material dating from 1896. NATPE Net, an electronic network for the entertainment industry, boasts databases with more than ten thousand radio and television stations. Firms like Accu-Weather offer local stations ready-for-air graphics. Federal databases can provide writers with government statistics that give stories greater depth.

This is a small sampling of available services. And the revolution has scarcely begun.

15. *What Else?*

Someone will ask, "What else? What little things, besides the rules, can you give me?" The person who asks that question wants inside information—the hot tips—on how a newswriter in this competitive business can succeed. What sets the best newswriters apart from the rest? Because this is a recurring question—and a good one—we'll try to answer it. The answer is based on firsthand experience. This isn't theory. It's what works.

Remember, we are assuming you know all the rules. So what we are talking about here are the extras, those additional, unprescribed things you do that make for a good script. These tips range from the quite profound—we aren't exaggerating—to those that may seem trivial, but they all matter.

• *Tip no. 1:* Care. Have a sense of caring. Shortly before Harry Reasoner died, Mike Wallace said, "He wasn't just a reporter getting a story. With Harry you got insight and compassion in addition to the facts." It's not enough to care about style. Care about the people in your story, whether it's an apartment house fire, yesterday's farm foreclosure, or last night's basketball game. Having compassion means caring about the tenants made homeless by the fire, the predicament of the farm family, the striving of individual players.

In a magical way, caring enhances writing. It affected Ed Murrow's broadcasts during the Battle of Britain, Walter Cronkite's reports on space exploration, Dan Rather's reporting from Tiananmen Square, and Peter Arnett's broadcasts from Baghdad. Not every story lends itself to this kind of involvement. It's hard to *feel* about an increase in the sewer tax. But always think about how what happened affects people.

• *Tip no. 2:* Be aware. If you are a good newswriter, you know what is happening in the city where you work and in the world. You read the newspapers and the newsmagazines. You listen to the news when you get up in the morning. You listen to the news in the car, and you listen to the news when you get home at night. You listen to the news just before you go to bed. You read all the wire copy you can get hold of while on the job.

The newswriter keeps informed. If you cannot stand the steady diet of news—if you aren't willing to prepare yourself for news writing, or reporting, to that extent—you should find other work. Top journalists brief themselves in this way as a matter of course. When they report for work they are ready for the *new* news of the day.

The writing staff of a station or network should be aware of the content of preceding newscasts. Often the writer can monitor programs by listening or watching in the newsroom. If this is not possible, you should read over the copy of the last broadcast to see which stories were used and how they were handled. In some newsrooms, the news editor decides what the lead story will be and what other stories should be reported. All this is necessary to avoid tiresome repetition, contradiction, and embarrassment in presenting news listeners already have heard as though it were brand new.

• *Tip no. 3:* If you write for an anchor, adapt your writing to his or her personality. Almost all newscasters write some of their stories. Notice how your newscaster writes. Some are more formal in their news presentation than others. Some go in for adjectives, for more color. Some like their stories to flow from one to the next with the help of transitional phrases. Some broadcasters don't mind long sentences, *if* the sentences are constructed for easy reading and easy comprehension. Some find it almost impossible to pronounce foreign names, so keep them to a minimum. But, most important, adapt your writing style to the broadcaster's style of writing. Be a copycat.

• *Tip no. 4:* Be creative. To do that, you have to think or, as Charles Osgood said, "engage your brain." When Connie Chung reported the development of an improved battery-powered car, she used the line "No gasoline to buy, just charge it." That's creative.

• *Tip no. 5:* Think what you are saying. Ask yourself, "Is this really what I want to say?" Next, ask yourself, "Will it be absolutely clear to the listener? Is there any danger of misinterpretation?" Now think another moment. "Am I saying something worded so clumsily as to make me look ridiculous?" Two examples:

A 15-year-old girl has won the right to play hockey with boys in Superior Court.

The priest was robbed and stabbed in his rectory.

• *Tip no. 6:* Don't waste time. Writing is a challenge (though it can be fun, too), and the writer who feels so confident of his ability that he kids around with co-workers for an hour or spends the hour in the cafeteria, because his broadcast isn't scheduled for another three hours, is guilty of overconfidence. Normally a five-minute newscast (which actually varies anywhere from three minutes to four and a half minutes, depending on commercials) requires an hour to write. Most news directors allow the writer an additional hour for reading the wires. Before beginning to write, a writer has to be "read in."

A few experienced professionals can write a five-minute newscast in twenty-five minutes. Others have trouble meeting the one-hour deadline. But the trick is to employ, usefully, *all* the time available. The writer cannot know what may happen to complicate his or her writing assignment. A late bulletin, some new leads, a story telephoned in by a reporter on the scene, or a call for help in editing a piece of tape or film—any number of things—can throw a writer off schedule. The time suddenly is gone. Earlier stories, no less important, are not written. News coverage suffers. Remember the fable of the tortoise and the hare. Don't dally. Stay on the job.

• *Tip no. 7:* Edit yourself. If you have time, rewrite. E. B. White's wife, Katherine, was an editor at *The New Yorker,* and she was also a very good writer. White said that "the editor in her fought the writer every inch of the way." Today, with so much live reporting, the editor in you has a more important role to play than ever before.

• *Tip no. 8:* This is a trick that works for newswriters in radio. (It's less applicable in television, where lines on the Tele-Promp-Ter are much shorter.) What it amounts to is linking one line of copy to the next by ending the first line with a word signaling continuity. For example, *the* is a good word to end a line with. It sends the reader chasing down to the next line for the word it modifies. The article *a* is just as good for the same reason. Prepositions and adjectives are useful, too, in this regard. So are conjunctions. But nouns are bad. They don't link. They do nothing to improve the flow of one line of copy to the next. You may think this is pretty fancy, but it's a trick one of the highest paid writers in the business has used.

• *Tip no. 9:* Don't overload your sentences. Here's an overloaded sentence: "She was a specialist who helped clients to fill out applications to determine their eligibility for assistance, including food stamps, aid to families with dependent children, and general public assistance." The litany of assistance programs should be shortened or unloaded into a second sentence. Do you see anything else that should be changed? You should. *To fill out applications to determine* is clumsy. (Two infinitives in succession almost always are.) So eliminate the word *to* in *to fill out.* It's superfluous. Now you have a cleaner, better-sounding sentence. Be ruthless. Kill any word or phrase that doesn't work for you.

• *Tip no. 10:* If possible, give your sentences strong endings—that is, end them with good, solid nouns or verbs. "After thinking it over, he decided not to run" is stronger and more effective than "He decided not to run after thinking it over." "For a year at least, the bank is safe" is a better sentence than "The bank is safe for a year at least." As David Brinkley said, "Never—*never*—end the sentence with a dependent clause. Get the trash out of the way first."

• *Tip no. 11:* Keep a dictionary handy. We would like to have a nickel for every "super" in which *sheriff* was misspelled. Other words commonly misspelled on the screen are *capital* and *capitol. Capital* is the city, *capitol* the building in which laws are passed. (One way to remember: picture the "o" in *capitol* as the dome.)

• *Tip no. 12:* This may be the most important tip. If you feel uneasy about any part of a story, if something doesn't seem quite right, check it out. Your gut feeling is a true friend.

A Final Word

We have come to the end of our instruction. The writing you will do—or are doing—is the most important writing in all of journalism. For news, the public relies most on radio and television—on you. We do not know you, but we know the responsibility you bear, and suspect you know it, too. We close with a few paragraphs from Eric Sevareid's last commentary for CBS evening news, which you might call his valedictory, and which he called his self-imposed rules of conduct as a broadcaster. These were:

> Not to underestimate the intelligence of the audience and not to overestimate its information.
>
> To remember always that the public is only people, and people only persons, no two alike.
>
> To retain the courage of one's doubts as well as one's convictions in this world of dangerously passionate certainties.
>
> To comfort oneself in times of error with the knowledge that the saving grace of the press—print or broadcast—is its self-correcting nature. And to remember that ignorant and biased reporting has its counterpart in ignorant and biased reading and listening. We do not speak into an intellectual or emotional void.

What the public must perceive in a broadcaster, he said, is "honesty and fair intent. There is in the American people a tough, undiminished instinct for what is fair."

George Polk was killed while on assignment in Greece. In a nationwide broadcast, Murrow spoke of Polk's reverence for fact. He said: "His stories stood up—every last one of them. He spared neither the corruption, inefficiency and petty political maneuvering of the Greek government, nor the vacillation of American policy, nor the atrocities committed by the Communists. What happened he reported, without fear and in language that all could understand."

The extra ingredient is integrity. It is honesty in seeking out and reporting the truth. And in radio and television especially, this must be done in language that all can understand.

Bibliography

Baker, Sheridan. *The Practical Stylist*. New York: Harper & Row, 1985.

Berner, R. Thomas. *Language Skills for Journalists*. Boston: Houghton Mifflin, 1979.

Bernstein, Theodore. *Watch Your Language*. New York: Atheneum, 1965.

——. *The Careful Writer*. New York: Atheneum, 1967.

——. *Miss Thistlebottom's Hobgoblins*. New York: Farrar, Straus and Giroux, 1974.

Bittner, John R. and Denise A. Bittner. *Radio Journalism*. Englewood Cliffs, N.J.: Prentice-Hall, 1977.

Bliss, Edward, Jr., ed. *In Search of Light: The Broadcasts of Edward R. Murrow, 1938–1961*. New York: Knopf, 1967; paperback, New York: Avon, 1974.

Block, Mervin. *Writing Broadcast News*. Chicago: Bonus Books, 1987.

——. *Rewriting Network News*. Chicago: Bonus Books, 1990.

Bremner, John. *Words on Words*. New York: Columbia University Press, 1981.

Brooks, Brian S. and James L. Pinson. *Working with Words: A Concise Handbook for Media Writers and Editors*. New York: St. Martin's, 1989.

Brooks, William F. *Radio News Writing*. New York: McGraw-Hill, 1948.

Broussard, E. Joseph and Jack F. Holgate. *Writing and Reporting Broadcast News*. New York: Macmillan, 1983.

Burchfield, Robert. *The Spoken Word: A BBC Guide*. New York: Oxford University Press, 1981.

Bush, Chilton R. *Newswriting and Reporting Public Affairs*. Philadelphia: Chilton, 1965.

Callihan, E. L. *Grammar for Journalists*, 3d ed. Radnor, Pa.; Chilton, 1979.

Cappon, Rene J. *The Word: An Associated Press Guide to Good Writing*. New York: Associated Press, 1982.

Chase, Stuart. *The Power of Words*. New York: Harcourt Brace and World, 1954.

Clark, Weaver J. *Broadcast Newswriting as Process*. New York: Longman, 1984.

Cohler, David Keith. *Broadcast Journalism: A Guide for the Presentation of Radio and Television News.* Englewood Cliffs, N.J.: Prentice-Hall, 1985.

——. *Broadcast Newswriting.* Englewood Cliffs, N.J.: Prentice-Hall, 1990.

Cook, Claire Kehrwald. *Line by Line: How to Edit Your Own Writing.* Boston: Houghton Mifflin, 1985.

Dary, David. *How to Write News for Broadcast and Print Media.* Blue Ridge Summit, Pa.: TAB Books, 1973.

Dudek, Lee J. *Professional Broadcast Announcing.* Boston: Allyn and Bacon, 1982.

Fang, Irving. *Those Radio Commentators!* Ames: Iowa State University Press, 1977.

——. *Television News/Radio News,* 4th ed. St. Paul: Rada Press, 1985.

Finn, Seth. *Broadcast Writing as a Liberal Art.* Englewood Cliffs, N.J.: Prentice Hall, 1991.

Flesch, Rudolf. *How to Write, Speak, and Think More Effectively,* Harper & Row, 1960.

——. *The Art of Readable Writing.* New York: Harper & Row, 1962.

Fowler, H. W. *Modern English Usage,* 2d ed. Revised by Sir Ernest Gowers. New York: Oxford University Press, 1985.

Garvey, Daniel and William L. Rivers. *Newswriting for the Electronic Media.* Belmont, Cal.: Wadsworth, 1982.

Garvey, Daniel and William L. Rivers. *Broadcast Writing.* New York: Longman, 1982.

Gibson, Roy. *Radio and Television Reporting.* Needham Heights, Mass.: Allyn and Bacon, 1991.

Green, Maury. *Television News: Anatomy and Process,* Belmont, Cal.: Wadsworth, 1969.

Greene, Robert S. *Television Writing.* New York: Harper & Row, 1956.

Hall, Mark. *Broadcast Journalism: An Introduction to News Writing,* 2d ed. New York: Hastings House, 1978.

Hausman, Carl. *Crafting the News for Electronic Media.* Belmont, Cal.: Wadsworth, 1992.

Hewitt, John. *Air Words: Writing for Broadcast News.* Mountain View, Cal.: Mayfair, 1988.

Hilliard, Robert L. *Writing for Radio and Television,* 5th ed. Belmont, Cal.: Wadsworth, 1991.

Hough, George A. *News Writing,* 4th ed. Boston: Houghton Mifflin, 1988.

Hunter, Julius K. and Lynne S. Gross. *Broadcast News: The Inside Out.* St. Louis: Mosby, 1980.

Itule, Bruce D. and Douglas Anderson. *Newswriting and Reporting for Today's Media.* New York: Random House, 1986.

Ives, Sumner. *A New Handbook for Writers.* New York: Knopf, 1960.

Jackson, Allan. *You Have to Write, Too!* Unpublished lecture, 1969.

Keith, Michael C. and Joseph M. Krause. *The Radio Station,* 3rd ed. Boston: Focal Press, 1993.

Kendrick, Alexander. *Prime Time: The Life of Edward R. Murrow.* Boston: Little, Brown, 1969.

Lambuth, David. *The Golden Book on Writing.* New York: Viking, 1964.

MacDonald, R. H. *A Broadcast News Manual of Style.* New York: Longman, 1987.

MacNeil, Robert. *Wordstruck.* New York: Viking, 1990.

Mayeux, Peter E. *Broadcast News Writing and Reporting.* Dubuque, Iowa: Brown, 1991.

Mencher, Melvin. *Basic News Writing,* 2d ed. Dubuque, Iowa: Brown, 1986.

——. *News Reporting and Writing,* 4th ed. Dubuque, Iowa: Brown, 1987.

Murrow, Edward R. *This Is London.* New York: Simon & Schuster, 1941.

Murrow, Edward R. and Fred W. Friendly. *See It Now.* Transcripts from "See It Now," edited by Murrow and Friendly. New York, Simon & Schuster, 1955.

Newman, Edwin. *Strictly Speaking,* New York: Bobbs-Merrill, 1974.

——. *A Civil Tongue.* New York: Bobbs-Merrill, 1976.

Papper, Robert. *Broadcast News Writing Stylebook.* Columbus, Ohio: Horizon, 1987.

Persico, Joseph E. *Edward R. Murrow: An American Original.* New York: McGraw-Hill, 1988.

Prato, Lou. *Covering the Environmental Beat.* Environmental Reporting Forum. Washington, D.C.: 1991.

Reasoner, Harry. *The Reasoner Report.* Garden City, N.Y.: Doubleday, 1966.

Sevareid, Eric. *In One Ear.* New York: Knopf, 1952.

——. *Small Sounds in the Night.* New York: Knopf, 1956.

Shirer, William L. *Berlin Diary.* New York: Knopf, 1941.

Shook, Frederick and Dan Lattimore. *The Broadcast News Process,* 4th ed. Englewood, Colo.: Morton, 1992.

Smeyak, G. Paul. *Broadcast News Writing.* Columbus, Ohio: Grid, 1977.

Sperber, A. M. *Murrow: His Life and Times.* New York: Freundlich Books, 1986.

Stahr, John. *Write to the Point.* New York: Macmillan, 1969.

Stein, M. L. *Write Clearly, Speak Effectively.* New York: Cornerstone Library, 1967.

Stephens, Mitchell. *Broadcast News,* 2d ed. New York: Rinehart and Winston, 1986.

Stovall, James. *Writing for the Mass Media.* Englewood Cliffs, N.J.: Prentice-Hall, 1985.

Strunk, William, Jr., and E. B. White. *The Elements of Style,* 3d ed. New York: Macmillan, 1979.

United Press International. *The U.P.I. Stylebook,* 3d ed. New York: U.P.I., 1992.

Utterback, Ann S. *Broadcast Voice Handbook.* Chicago: Bonus Books, 1990.

Walters, Roger. *Broadcast Writing: Principles and Practice.* New York: 1987.

Weaver, J. Clark. *Broadcast Newswriting as a Process.* New York: Longman, 1984.

Weaver, Luther. *The Technique of Radio Writing.* Englewood Cliffs, N.J.: Prentice-Hall, 1948.

White, Paul W. *News on the Air.* New York: Harcourt, Brace, 1947.

White, Ted, Adrian J. Meppen, and Steve Young. *Broadcast News Writing, Reporting, and Production.* New York: Macmillan, 1984.

Willis, Edgar E. *Writing Television and Radio Programs.* New York: Holt, Rinehart and Winston, 1967.

Wimer, Arthur and Dale Brix. *Workbook for Radio and TV News Editing and Writing,* 4th ed. Dubuque, Iowa: Brown, 1976.

Wood, William A. *Electronic Journalism.* New York: Columbia University Press, 1967.

Wulfemeyer, K. Tim. *Broadcast Newswriting: A Workbook.* Ames, Iowa: Iowa State University Press, 1983.

——. *Beginning Broadcast Newswriting,* 2d ed. Ames, Iowa: Iowa State University Press, 1984.

Yoakam, Richard and Charles F. Cremer, eds. *ENG: Television News and the New Technology,* 2d ed. New York: Random House, 1989.

York, Ivor. *The Technique of Television News.* Boston: Focal Press, 1987.

Zinsser, William. *On Writing Well,* 3d ed. New York: Harper & Row, 1985.

Zousmer, Steven. *TV News Off-Camera: An Insider's Guide to Newswriting and Newspeople.* Ann Arbor: University of Michigan Press, 1987.

Index

Text: 10/13.3 Times Roman

Compositor: Maple-Vail

Printer: Maple-Vail

Binder: Maple-Vail